8 PARADOXES

of

LEADERSHIP AGILITY

8 PARADOXES

of

LEADERSHIP AGILITY

How to lead and inspire in the real world

YEO CHUEN CHUEN

ACESENCE

ACESENCE

Published by ACESENCE
Singapore

ISBN 978-981-14-5846-0

© 2019 ACESENCE
First Edition 2019
Second Edition 2020

Disclaimer: We support the copyright of all intellectual property. Copyright protection protects creativity and ensures the voices of content producers are rightfully acknowledged.

This publication is intended to provide helpful and informative material. It is not intended to diagnose, treat, cure, or prevent any health problem or condition, nor is it intended to replace the advice of physicians or qualified healthcare professionals. No action should be taken solely based on the contents of this book. Always consult your physician or qualified healthcare professional on any matter regarding your health and before adopting suggestions in this book, whether written or inferred.

The author and publisher expressly disclaim all responsibility for any liability, loss or risk, personal or otherwise, incurred as a consequence, directly or indirectly, from the use or application of any contents of this book. Any and all product names referenced within this book are the trademark of their respective owners. None of these owners have sponsored, authorized, endorsed, or approved this book.

Always read all information provided by the manufacturers' product labels before using their products. The author and publisher are not responsible for claims made by manufacturers.

TESTIMONIALS

This book takes a pragmatic approach and gives a real-world perspective on issues faced by leaders today.

The examples are lively and relevant. They are highly useful for me as I coach my first-line managers.

As part of my coaching program, I read Chuen Chuen's *8 Paradoxes of Leadership Agility.* Just from two chapters, I could immediately see real-life connections with the paradoxes mentioned. The reflection questions helped me source new solutions. This book is a must-read for leaders.

This book showed me how I can lead with strategies – how to speak with employees, clients, and partners.

A real page-turner, it's very insightful without being too theoretical.

I saw myself in the characters of your book. It was as though I was reliving my journey and reflecting on leadership.

This book highlights surprising but real paradoxes all leaders will encounter and tough choices they will have to make in approaching, leading or coaching transformations.

It's great to have a book that acknowledges and provides insights to paradoxes. Well worth the read.

After reading an excerpt, I decided this was one book I wanted to read. Many books I buy remain unread, but not this one. The concise, easy-to-digest style appealed as did the opportunity to understand paradoxes faced by others.

The book lived up to expectations. Once I started, I could not put it down and finished it in one afternoon. Section I sets the scene. Section II went over the eight paradoxes with just the right amount of detail, with a specific case study for each. Information was presented in clear and consistent sections.

The exercises are nicely packaged in Section III with more detailed explanations for those who want to delve deeper. This meant I could swiftly go through the first two sections knowing I could explore further if needed.

Chuen Chuen's book was engaging, relevant and enlightening. Drawing from her coaching journey, she succinctly described common challenges faced by leaders, fleshed out the paradoxes faced, and demonstrated how she successfully coached her clients through the Re4 Coaching Model. A book that will yield much insights, and which I highly recommended!

ALVIN TAN, HEAD OF STRATEGY, PARTNERSHIPS & BUSINESS DEVELOPMENT, SINGAPORE

Many leaders will find this book useful as it shows them, in a structured way, how they can become agile in an increasingly complex environment.

NEO LEY LEE, DIRECTOR, FINANCIAL ADVISORY, SINGAPORE

It's really practical, and I can relate to the characters in the book. I highly recommend this book because it provides deep insights.

CHRISTIAN KASTNER, SALES DIRECTOR, GERMANY

A highly readable and practical book. To help readers better understand the concepts of paradoxes, Chuen Chuen starts each chapter with a story in the workplace featuring a protagonist from her coaching assignment. Then she shows us a framework to address the predicaments faced by each character and demonstrates how we too can use the framework in our situations. Useful guide.

EARN MENG CHAN, HR DIRECTOR, SINGAPORE

Great eye-opener. This book stood out as it broke down what leadership is all about.

DARYL CHEW, REGIONAL INFORMATION SECURITY OFFICER, SINGAPORE

This is a book I would recommend. The language is kept simple, and there are ample real-life stories that make the principles very relatable.

I especially like how Chuen Chuen used metaphors with clients to help them put their finger on a complex situation in a simple way. This simplicity and clarity are needed more than ever before especially in this age of information overload. Chuen Chuen meticulously documented her experiences with each client for each paradox, making their real-life stories practical guides for leaders who want to navigate the paradoxes they face.

There are many leadership books out there that are heavy on concept and light on real-world application. This is NOT one of those books. In *8 Paradoxes of Leadership Agility* the author outlines the eight distinct paradoxes and then shares real-life stories of a leadership issue, the featured leader's challenges, the process for deriving a solution, and the outcome. The way in which it is written gives you the sense that you are in the room with the author and each leader. This book has depth, detail, and something all leaders can learn from to make themselves, their workplace, and their teams better.

Out of numerous leadership books I've read, this one stood out by turning real-time experiences into pages.

The technique of using metaphors to change mindsets is fascinating as it helps people explore ideas in a new light, in a way that appeals to the emotional and creative side of the brain.

The case studies are practical and relatable. The paradoxes help us be open-minded and flexible, and encourage us to have balanced thinking. Our strengths might become weaknesses if we overuse them or fail to keep them in balance with other perspectives. I recommend leaders grab this book and gain new perspectives from it. It will open readers' minds to different dimensions; and leaders should not be constrained within certain leadership styles.

The book amazed and intrigued me, and made me think deeply about every paradox.

This book inspired me to learn from my past experiences and embrace being a task-oriented and people-oriented leader.

Scan this code to tune in to podcasts where Chuen Chuen interviews many of these thought-leaders on their real-world insights.

https://blog.acesence.com/category/agile-leaders-conversations/

CONTENTS

ACKNOWLEDGMENTS

Writing a book was never my intention. In fact, I ran from the idea and pushed it to the back of my mind. My focus was to support leaders in their growth through personal coaching.

One day, I looked back at all the learning I had gained from my clients and realized that putting those insights into a book would make a lot of sense. A book could potentially extend the benefits of this learning beyond the limited numbers I could personally coach.

Hence, this book was birthed.

This endeavour would not have been possible without the support and contribution of the many who gifted me with their wisdom, insights and generous sharing.

I would like to acknowledge my family, friends, clients, coaches, mentors and partners who made this journey so much more delightful.

Special thanks to my clients and partners who reviewed my manuscript, gave invaluable feedback and helped sharpen my thinking.

I also wish to thank the many leadership gurus who have influenced my work, for without you, I would have remained the same, a 'frog in the well'. Without you, my life would not have truly begun.

Finally, thank you, my reader, for buying and reading this book. Your support is so important to me.

FOREWORD TO SECOND EDITION

Continuous improvement is my guiding principle. I have always believed there's a higher peak to scale.

Since the launch of my ebook in early March 2020 on Amazon, it has reached the #1 spot in New Releases in various categories and remained there for a considerable amount of time. I received heartening affirmation from readers who found the stories and coaching model practical, useful and inspirational.

Along with that, I also received insightful suggestions from discerning readers on how I could make this book even better. I am deeply grateful that readers took the time to send me their suggestions. So *violà*! This second edition is born!

In this brand new edition, the core explanations on the Re4 Coaching Model as well as the Re4 Coaching Model Exercises remain unchanged. But the writing is now more succinct and direct.

I have clarified explanations so readers can immediately capture the essence of the learning and put them to good use.

In the spirit of agility, I have also been in the process of updating and refreshing ACESENCE, my flagship brand. This second edition, therefore, has a fresh new design, aligned to the new brand image.

Once again, my heartfelt gratitude goes to my supporters and readers who shared their input on the first edition. If you like this new edition, have suggestions on its improvement, or have new paradoxes you want to share with me, please write to me at *chuenchuen@ACESENCE.com*. I look forward to hearing from you.

FOREWORD

BY SUNIL MUNDRA

We are currently in VUCA times, i.e., in times of Volatility, Uncertainty, Complexity and Ambiguity. For leaders, these manifest in having to deal with too many unknowns, non-linearity between cause and effect, unintended and often undesirable consequences after interventions, and plans falling apart quickly due to fast-paced changes, to name a few. This is diametrically different from an environment which was largely certain and predictable, which prevailed for decades.

Consequently, leaders need to make a marked shift in their mindset and behaviours to deal with VUCA. And one of those shifts is how they deal with paradoxes.

A paradox is the simultaneous existence of two opposite or contradictory ideas, both being valid and interrelated (e.g. short vs. long term, global vs. local, etc).

In a VUCA environment, it is important for leaders to approach paradoxes by accepting the tension between contradictions and competing demands. This allows the situations to unfold and results in greater flexibility and creativity in decision making. This is very different from approaching paradoxes like problems and solving in favour of only one dimension at the cost of the other. Such an approach might work in a predictable and certain environment but could be disastrous under VUCA conditions.

Chuen Chuen's book is therefore so timely and apt, given that VUCA is for real for enterprises, regardless of size, industry or geography. She has addressed eight paradoxes, which are very relevant and relatable. For each of the eight paradoxes, she has explained what the paradox is about and brought each one to life through stories using specific leader personas.

She has provided critical insights about each paradox by sharing the reflections of the personas. The most valuable part of the book is that she prompts the readers with some pointed questions to reflect about the paradox in their context. This will enable the leaders to absorb the learnings from the book in a very effective way.

The book is lucid, focused and thought provoking. It is a must read for leaders as it will help them to embrace the paradox mindset, which is a critical capability to deal with VUCA.

Sunil Mundra
ORGANISATIONAL CHANGE AND TRANSFORMATION LEADER,
CXO ADVISOR @ THOUGHTWORKS
AUTHOR OF 'ENTERPRISE AGILITY - BEING AGILE IN A CHANGING WORLD

INTRODUCTION

I wrote this book for leaders who want to be different. Effective. Agile. Leaders who, having read countless books on leadership, still wonder how principles can be put to use in the real world. This book bridges the gap between theory and practice.

In these pages, I share a collection of paradoxes I gleaned from years of encounters with people I have coached, many of whom are leaders in Fortune 500 companies. You will read about their conundrums and how I applied the Re4 Coaching Model — a model I created and refined — to help them navigate their paradoxes and reach their goals.

While key milestones of each client's story are preserved, names, industries, demographics and specificities of each situation have been changed to ensure confidentiality. What matters is not the 'who' in these stories, but the learning that we can all derive from their experiences.

The Re4 Coaching Model does not offer a one-size-fits-all solution, but rather, an approach that supports individuals to reach solutions that work uniquely for them, in both personal and professional contexts.

You will find a structured, supportive framework through which newfound insights can be acted upon. The learning will enable you to harness the all-important asset of every leader — an agile mindset. It will give you the essential advantage to lead with confidence, certainty and impact in this volatile, uncertain, complex and often ambiguous world.

The road to leadership agility is a paradoxical one. This book, by no means, addresses all possible paradoxes. So, if you encounter a new paradox which you wish to share, or find yourself mired in one and want to work on it together, or simply want to accelerate your leadership growth, you can reach me easily through LinkedIn or by email at ***chuenchuen@ACESENCE.com***. I will be pleased to connect with you.

How to use this book

This book has three parts.

PART I   This sets the foundations of leadership agility.

PART II   Here, real-life stories packed with essential learning illustrate the eight paradoxes and show how my clients used the proprietary Re4 Coaching Model to navigate each paradox successfully and make vital mindset shifts.

PART III   This provides the comprehensive reflections of individuals featured in Part II, illustrating how they applied the Re4 Coaching Model. Re4 Coaching Model Exercises are also given here for your use, so you can work through the paradoxes which resonate with you. (Printable PDF templates of these exercises can be downloaded; simply scan the QR code on page 87.)

I wish you every success as a leader of agility.

PART I

LEADERSHIP AGILITY & THE NEED FOR CHANGE

AGILITY AND CHANGE

What is agility?

Definitions of agility abound in business writing and other literature. One definition I found helpful was that agility is the ability to take wise, effective action amid complex, rapidly changing conditions (Joiner, Josephs, 2007).

My definition of agility is drawn from years of coaching practice and from the success stories of the multinational clients and organizations with whom I have worked. From these experiences, I have concluded that:

> *Agility is about the ability*
> *to flexibly navigate*
> *uncertainties and complexities*
> *while maintaining*
> *a sense of ease and authenticity.*

It involves changing while not losing one's bearings, being rooted while spreading out, remaining true to one's self while adapting to new circumstances.

Agility is a mindset, the way one thinks. We do not become agile by following frameworks, models or protocols.

Agility is a critical leadership mindset to develop, and indeed to embrace, in our lives and careers. After all, leadership is often exercised in complicated, seemingly contradictory circumstances, and in ever-shifting contexts.

Change is difficult and often paradoxical

I was an educator — had been for over a decade — when I discovered my love for coaching. I had always been an advocate of lifelong learning and leadership development as an educator, but my life took a turn when I attended a world-class leadership conference one day in August of 2012. In a hall filled with 800 other people, I sat transfixed as Dr John Maxwell's voice filled the room. Something magical happened. I felt as if I was the only person in the hall. Leaning in on his every word, I drank in his message about living my life to fulfill a purpose and a mission. A dream took hold of me that day. I would become a renowned professional coach!

Five years into coaching, I tasted a little of the life of which I had dreamed. But I kept at bay the notion of starting a business as I clung to the stability that a regular job offered. I am grateful for friends who, in the early days of my coaching practice, spared precious time to give me hours of practice. My hard work and their 'sacrifice' paid off as my coaching skills rapidly improved. In hindsight, this was perhaps the greatest factor for my success as a professional coach. I spent a considerable amount of time acquiring broad knowledge on psychology, business, organizational expertise and honing my skills in coaching using the competency model by the Executive Coaching Forum (2008).

After those initial years of intensive practice, I was propelled to the next level when I was engaged to coach the senior leadership of the United Nations. All these transformations took place while I remained cocooned in the safety of my full-time job as an educator.

But all the while, thoughts of running my own coaching practice continued to play in my mind, especially with each successive heart-lifting testimonial from clients all over the world, detailing how my coaching had catalyzed immense growth in their careers. I remember one person especially, a country director of an office in Southeast Asia. After my first session with her, a long gap ensued. In the silence, self-doubt began to assail me. Had she disengaged from me because of poor chemistry between us? Was I lacking in my skills?

My fears vanished when she reconnected to complete the coaching engagement. She revealed that our first session together was pivotal for her and gave her the strength to pull through a very difficult transition. This validation egged me closer to the precipice of starting my own coaching practice. But doubt whispered: "No, it's too risky… How will I pay the bills if my income is unstable? … It's impossible. How will people know of me amongst the sea of good coaches out there?"

As you read this, you can probably see that I was trapped by my need for security. The longer I stayed in my secure and stable job, the more difficult it was to make the change. At the same time, the desire to make my dream a reality burned stronger. The pressure of two opposing forces clashed and tugged against each other, pulling me in opposite directions. Before me lay two paths: leave the job security and plunge headlong into the dream of becoming a professional coach, or cling to job security and give up my dream of coaching full-time and connecting with inspiring world leaders.

My heart was calling out, "Dare to pursue your dream! Throw caution to the wind!" But my head said, "Stay safe! Don't take risks!" To move on and create the life I had envisioned for myself, I had to silence this internal war. I needed to resolve this paradox of 'being bold' versus 'being safe'. I had to identify what changes I was willing to make and start taking action to bring me closer to the career of my dreams. To change, I had to morph and be agile, to think, feel and act differently. Does my story resonate with you?

*In which area of your life
do you long for change?*

The price of not changing

Having coached clients from more than 30 countries, I recognize a theme that recurs, though circumstances may differ. It usually plays out like this: A high-performing individual receives promotion to a leadership position based on the merit of achievements or contributions. In the new role, however, this person continues to rely on familiar methods that used to bring success. The individual does not realize that these methods do not work in the new role and may, in fact, be the cause of failure or decline in this new circumstance.

This leader demonstrates a lack of agility in the midst of change. Even while correctly identifying the fork in the road, this individual usually finds justifications that prevent him from adjusting (Jensen, 2013). Here is a typical story.

Jane, a high performer, had won her superiors over with her excellent execution and implementation. She was decisive, sharp and quick. She had an eye for detail and enjoyed her work tremendously. Having proven herself an invaluable asset to her organization, Jane's success at work fed her self-worth. She was the typical overachiever. Being average was not an option.

In recognition of her stellar performance, Jane was promoted to team leader. She quickly made her expectations known to her team — being average was not an option. She felt this was reasonable as it was no less than what she expected of herself. She confronted team members who 'dropped the ball'. She wanted to be involved in everything and to the most minute detail as she wanted her team to get every minutiae exactly right.

Months later, a few of her team members, including some high performers, decided to leave the company. Jane's leadership style was one key reason cited for their departure. Alerted that there may be a problem, the management called Jane's remaining team members in for a focus group discussion to gather feedback on Jane's leadership. This was what they heard:

"I could not get my ideas across. Jane just wanted everything her way. There was no room for any voice other than hers."

"I missed a detail and Jane got really worked up. I didn't think it was that critical. When everything seems important and urgent, I don't know where to focus. I feel so overwhelmed."

Jane's superiors delivered the feedback to her about her leadership style and gave her three months to get her act together. As part of the intervention, Jane decided to engage a coach on her own accord and this was how we started working together.

At our first session, I saw that Jane was burnt out from trying to get her team to live up to her expectations to be 'mini-Janes'. We talked about her aspiration to be a great leader. She soon realized that she was using an old definition of what a 'great leader' was and that it was no longer relevant in her new context.

Jane had a choice — stay the same and return to her former position — or be agile and work on changes that could make her more successful in leading her team.

If you were Jane, which
would you choose?

LEARNING TO BE AGILE

A well-meaning mentor may tell you that to be successful, you need to be agile. Agility is a much-talked-about, crucial quality expected of leaders, like strategic thinking. It is not, however, a switch we can flip 'on' or 'off' at will.

How then does a leader become agile? How can a leader lead effectively in a volatile, uncertain, complex and ambiguous environment? The truth is, without agility, it will be impossible to go in the 'right' direction, or any direction at all (Kotter, 2014). But how will a leader know what to do? Are there 'signposts' to follow?

Change is the only constant

A good starting point will be to recognize that parameters are ever-changing and that definitions change with them. Diversity in teams has become increasingly complex with a blending of nationalities, cultures, faiths, genders and beliefs. The 'bottom line' for businesses has changed too. What used to work can be surprisingly ineffective or unexpectedly adequate.

Next, leaders need to understand that the process of becoming agile is a continuous journey. Agility is a mindset; it does not have a destination. Start examining the 'signposts' and be ready to take actions different from what you are familiar with. You might have heard the saying — to keep on doing the same thing while expecting a different result is insanity. And this is true.

What can you do to achieve a different outcome?

Fly the plane while we build it

A leader with whom I used to work once said, "Let's fly the plane while we build it." The journey to becoming agile is exactly the same.

To be an agile leader, what is first needed is a shift from a 'fixed' to 'growth' mindset (Dweck, 2006), which means being willing to accept truths contrary to the ones to which you are accustomed. Next, you need to take a good inward look at your authentic self.

Who are you really?

If you were to describe yourself using a metaphor, what would you choose? Would you be an eagle, a dolphin or a tortoise? Do you know your limits — what you can and cannot do; what you will or will not change?

Being agile does not mean throwing out everything from your past. It does mean being selective and discerning about what to preserve — traditions that are still meaningful and serve a purpose — and to re-innovate paradigms that no longer work. These changes may take time, but they all begin with this step of asking yourself:

1. What does agility mean to me?
2. How agile is my mind? To which ideals am I clinging?
3. What will happen if I stay unchanged?
4. What is an area that I cannot or will not change?
5. What is an area in which I must not stay unchanged?
6. What am I willing to experiment with to start changing?

Re4 Coaching Model

To support my clients' transition to becoming agile leaders, I use the Re4 Coaching Model, a proprietary model I developed and refined over the years. It has yielded results every time.

In this book, I share how you can use this Re4 Coaching Model to embark on the road to agility for yourself and those you lead.

Four steps of the Re4 Coaching Model

STEP 1
RECONSTRUCT THE MAP

An unbiased, courageous reality check, leading to a recognition of the truths in the context, which are likely different from how they were initially perceived.

STEP 2
REFRESH THE LENS

Uncover and weed out biases, prejudices or over-generalized rules that are no longer effective, leading to an internal shift of mindset.

STEP 3
RENEW THE IDENTITY

The shift is made explicit. It comes alive as the individual entrenches it using an anchoring metaphor that points to a new persona.

STEP 4
REBUILD THE CAPABILITIES

New skills and actions are learned, acquired and practiced, leading to improved outcomes.

WHEN STRESSED, LOOK FOR CLUES

Good stress, bad stress

Without a doubt, we all face challenges. Some difficulties push us toward higher goals. Others beat us up and leave us breathless in a corner of the ring. Whether we feel we are winning or losing, all challenges have this in common — stress. Stress because what we used to know no longer works. Stress because what we feel like doing is the opposite of what our minds are screaming for us to do. Stress because we fear what others might think, or even how we feel about ourselves.

I recall a conversation I had with an esteemed colleague in my first career as a teacher in a middle school. It had been a particularly hectic day. To regain my sanity, I self-declared a midday tea break at a nearby coffee shop where, in the company of this wise old gentleman who had seen his share of good and bad days, I poured out my complaints. Sipping a comforting cup of tea, I lamented how stressful life had become — students were having a tough time managing pressures from home, school, themselves, peers, and so on. I was suffering from the anxiety of having to cater to this diverse group of 'clients'.

My colleague looked back at me. His silver-grey mustache twitched as he smiled and said, "Chuen Chuen, we are molding the lives of students, as well as our own lives. You and I understand that just the right amount of pressure can turn ordinary clay into useful pottery or even a piece of art." I blinked as I considered his words. Seeing my receptiveness, he delivered his punchline,

"Stress can be bad, but if used right, we can create something useful, something beautiful."

*Stress, when correctly applied, can be
a powerful force in shaping our lives.*

When stress becomes unbearable, or when we are in a long stasis without any stress at all, it is time to reexamine our lives and make adjustments to regain the balance of just the right amount of stress.

Stress as a signal

Stress is inevitable in our often fast-paced, uncertain and complex lives. Most of us spend 40 to 50 years in economically productive but stressful careers. Living with stress, however, is not only inevitable but necessary. We cannot beat stress, we cannot escape it, and most definitely, we cannot ignore it.

Let us acknowledge that stress is a constant companion. What if stress is not a harmful companion but one which comes to deliver a message? Just as aches and pains in the body often indicate underlying issues such as physical imbalances, emotional tensions or trauma, stress also signals something.

*What are the clues you can look for
to identify the causes of stress in your life?*

Paradoxes

Since stress is inevitable, we need to learn to determine its sources. From the stories of my clients, I was able to identify a pattern typical of stressful situations. Most often I hear clients saying they "don't know what to make of things", "don't know how else to proceed", "hear the head saying something but the gut saying something else". These are all telltale signs of unresolved paradoxes.

Interestingly, these paradoxes have common themes and can be classified into similar categories, irrespective of differences in nationalities, cultures, ages, genders, academic and industry backgrounds. From senior leaders in top banks to managing directors of pharmaceutical conglomerates, from executives of start-ups to those of Fortune 500 companies, these paradoxes are present, albeit in vastly different circumstances.

When I listen to clients relate about stressful events or situations, I listen for the conflicts within them. Beneath the calm, professional façade, I can hear underlying tension, ready to overflow. From their voices, I pick up the energy with which they speak, how they emphasize certain words or phrases. I observe their gestures and how they present themselves from week to week. These are clues that announce the presence of unwanted stress. Their discomfort at being stuck in situations or mired in uncertainty tells me a paradox is present.

So, what are paradoxes?

When opposing states are right

Here, I define a paradox as a situation where two opposing states are both correct at the same time and where neither is superior to the other.

Faced with a paradox, how does one decide which side to lean toward? Well, that all depends on you and your situation. What is right in one instance, may be wrong in another. For instance, does a company need creativity or structure? Can a company be successful with 100 percent creativity and 0 percent structure? Can the reverse be true?

Generally, creativity and structure are very much intertwined and one cannot exist without the other. I have encountered situations, however, where too much creativity or too much structure becomes a liability.

Since both are right, the combination of creativity and structure has to be just right for the best results to happen. So the right question to ask is not which is right, but how much of each is needed in a particular situation.

Paradoxes can be challenging to embrace and accept as many of us received our education in systems where absoluteness and certainty are valued.

As a trained computer engineer, this logical side of my brain is certainly well-developed. I was fortunate that I had a strong background in the arts through music, which kept the other side of my brain active. However, my need to satisfy the logical mind and its need for absoluteness were challenges I had to deal with in the past.

Bright-eyed and hopeful, I expected that Action A would result in Output 1, and Action B, would yield Output 2. Simple, right? Imagine my horror when I realized that the real world did not work according to my expectations! Between 'black' and 'white', I found infinite shades of 'grey' (or any other color for that matter).

As I became a veteran in the workplace, I began to see that paradoxes exist everywhere. It is often not 'black versus white', but 'a shade of white versus another shade of white', where seemingly opposite sides are 'right'. And everything in between is also correct. This makes operating in any business context complex and full of uncertainty.

So what can we do?

Check your inner compass

Let's take a look at what happens when you face a paradox.

Imagine you are standing between opposing sides of a paradox. If you lean too much to one side, you start to feel the pull from the opposite end. The further you lean toward one side, the stronger the opposing pull tries to draw you back. The tension is only relieved when you manage to perfectly balance the pull from both ends.

And does perfect balance mean you are standing in the middle? No, it does not!

The state of balance is different for each person and for each circumstance. What is right for one may be different for another, depending on his or her upbringing, experiences, values and beliefs.

I like to think of our self-awareness of what is important to us as an inner compass. If you lack clarity about what is important to you and why it is important, then it will be difficult to make decisions or take action.

This is why, the first stage of my work with clients is to uncover, realign and reaffirm their values and beliefs. This vital step in our coaching partnership lays a solid foundation for all other work that flows after it. My promise to clients who have chosen to work with me is: "I cannot make your problems go away, but I can guarantee that you will respond with greater speed, accuracy and authenticity."

We live in volatile times. Nothing is ever certain. No one can predict our tomorrows. If you have succeeded once, there is no guarantee of success the next time. The only thing we can be certain of is the inner compass that guides our thoughts, feelings and actions.

Once my clients find that inner compass that uniquely characterizes them, they can find the perfect balance that is right only for them within that paradox.

Are you in a paradox now?

Remember, stress can clue you in about a possible paradox in your life. Ask yourself:

1. How much stress do I feel now?
2. Is this stress good or bad? If it is bad, what do I need to change to be in balance?
3. What am I feeling conflicted about?
4. If I am on a line with two opposing ends (white versus another shade of white), where do I stand now?

In the next part of this book, we look at eight common paradoxes and how to achieve the state of balance using the Re4 Coaching Model.

PART II

THE EIGHT PARADOXES

The 'paradox' is only
a conflict between reality
and your feeling of what
reality 'ought to be'.

Richard P. Feynman

PARADOX 1
TASKS vs PEOPLE

SERENE
A high potential aspiring to the next level of leadership

"I just received my 360 assessment report, and honestly, I am not convinced that I have been fairly assessed," frowned Serene as we began our fortnightly session.

Serene, a high performer in a global technology company, worked in a multinational team with a manager and three teammates. All of them were located in regional offices across different time zones.

A go-getter and eyes-on-the-ball type of leader, Serene was someone her manager and teammates could count on to deliver results, on time and on target. She took pride in being seen as a person who always met objectives and pushed her product line to the next level.

Serene participated in a 360 assessment implemented as part of a leadership development program in her company. The feedback that came through that assessment, however, caught her completely off-guard. She had always thought her interactions with her manager and her team were cordial, so she was not prepared for the critique she received. To her dismay, her professional image had been perceived as being less-than-perfect.

This was how we started working together.

<u>Serene's goals:</u>
To develop her career, see growth in scope
and an increase in responsibilities

As we discussed specific feedback in the report, a theme began to emerge. Serene's manager and coworkers consistently found her rigid in the way she managed projects. She consistently ignored the 'softer' aspects of working relations, often curtly rejecting requests that could compromise deadlines and outcomes.

Her teammates found it difficult to work with her, especially when negotiations were involved. Arranging meetings was a particular pain as Serene would only take calls during her office hours. She was described as being transactional and 'by-the-book'. On the dimension of 'being an inspiration', her scores were much lower than she had expected. In fact, her manager and coworkers described her as being cold and uninterested in building relationships with them despite having worked together for years.

At first, Serene defensively refuted all the feedback and found a justification for every comment. She saw only the good in being business-like, transactional and even curt where deadlines were concerned. She reasoned that the high-performance rating she had earned in the past four years was due to her hawk-like focus on meeting deadlines and maintaining high-quality outcomes at all costs.

Serene was faced with a paradox. She had to make some choices.

It was now necessary for Serene to leverage the findings
from the report to help her reach her goals sooner.

TASKS vs PEOPLE

In this paradox, leaders are challenged by the fact that their performance is measured by the 'hard' facts of results as well as the equally important 'softer' intangibles of relationships. While most leaders understand that tangible outcomes and quality of relationships are intertwined, they struggle to see that results alone are not enough to prove their leadership mettle.

I attribute this to a culture that values being 'rational' over being 'emotional'. In this culture, we usually suppress, dismiss or downplay our feelings, displacing them with rational evidence.

Despite achieving solid results, many clients found that being 'rational' only got them to a certain point. Based on the merit of achievements, they were promoted ahead of their peers. But once they started leading teams, their careers stalled. In these cases, feedback from coworkers typically depicted a cold, transactional leadership style where nothing seemed to matter more than tasks and numbers. What the leader regarded as 'drive' was seen by coworkers as trampling over people to get results.

The leader might think he had won many battles if he looked just at hard numbers. But if he evaluated staff morale and climate, he might realize that he lost the war. There is no victory if people lose faith and trust, or feel used.

To achieve a state of balance in this paradox, a leader needs to focus on both 'tasks' and 'people'. Achieve results in alignment with company goals while nurturing relationships. Make working together a rewarding experience and share the fruits of success.

SERENE'S JOURNEY

THROUGH THE RE4 COACHING MODEL

STEP 1
RECONSTRUCT THE MAP

**The strengths of Serene's working
style hindered her career progression.**

STEP 2
REFRESH THE LENS

**To grow in her career, Serene needed to
build relationships with her stakeholders.**

STEP 3
RENEW THE IDENTITY

**With her roots strongly developed,
she was ready now to cast her influence
far and wide, like a dandelion.**

STEP 4
REBUILD THE CAPABILITIES

**Serene committed to building
relationships while staying true to herself.**

(Serene's comprehensive reflections can be found on pages 89 to 96.)

STEP 1: RECONSTRUCT THE MAP

By taking an objective look at reality, Serene realized the main reason she was goal-driven and focused on completing work within deadlines was to protect her time with her family.

She saw how this laser-focused drive had benefited her family life and had even built her a solid reputation in her organization over the years. The upside was that she had a great family life and had been able to move projects quickly at work. The downside was that her career might stagnate if she continued working this way, especially in the way she interacted.

STEP 2: REFRESH THE LENS

Serene became aware of her strong aspirations to grow in both scope and responsibilities in her company. When she recognized that building good relations with key stakeholders could make a significant and positive difference to her career, she committed to changing how she had been working with and relating to colleagues.

STEPS 3 & 4: RENEW THE IDENTITY & REBUILD THE CAPABILITIES

Serene used to see herself as a small, insignificant plant though her roots were firmly and deeply rooted. The deep roots represented her commitment to her family. Now she embraced a new metaphor — that of a dandelion. Still rooted in her love for family, she was now ready to increase her circle of influence, like the seeds of the dandelion carried far and wide by the wind.

Serene put her creativity to good use and identified ways to build relationships with coworkers despite the distances. Through some reframing we did together, she saw that staying true to her need for speed and responsiveness did not mean sacrificing diplomacy.

Serene committed to taking these actions:

1. Make small talk at the start of every conference call to build rapport with the team.
2. Build relationships with stakeholders by communicating appropriately.
3. Stay true to herself; be firm about deadlines, but with diplomacy.

Serene's new narrative for success

When I met Serene a few weeks later, she appeared more relaxed. Happier. I noticed she had her hair newly coiffed! The image she projected was positive, warm even.

She told me she had completed all the actions and was able to maintain important deadlines. She also realized she used to reply curtly to emails when she responded to them immediately, so she decided to delay replying for at least 12 hours. This allowed her to distance herself and give a more considered response, especially in situations where she felt emotionally triggered. Serene found that this pause allowed her to consider other perspectives which sometimes caused her to change her initial decisions. She was happy to report that her new attitude was well-received by her colleagues.

Some months later, to my surprise, she went so far as to offer time for meetings with colleagues at their convenience, while she was on an extended holiday. Her colleagues became even more understanding and accommodating toward her as they appreciated this effort she made to be available to them while on holiday. She then had the best of both worlds — her family and professional life were harmonized. At the end of our coaching engagement,

Serene earned a new job scope and
the role of a people-leader.

Teams are made of individuals. When you focus on teams, individuality is diluted. When you focus on individuals, the team loses its identity.

PARADOX 2
INDIVIDUALS vs TEAMS

TIM

A veteran team leader whose
leadership came into question

"I am spending so much time coaching Ryan, I am neglecting my work! I don't know what else I can do to help him perform better," sighed Tim. "I am not looking forward to the next conversation with my manager. She has been harping on Ryan's poor work performance in our past three meetings. If this goes on any longer, my year-end performance rating will be affected. They are using Ryan's poor performance as an indicator of my leadership abilities!" Tim said, his tone rising in agitation.

Tim was a veteran manager handling a large team. Originally from an established local IT setup in Asia, Tim had always managed relationships with superiors, colleagues and subordinates well. Tim's huge success attracted the attention of a global IT company that had just penetrated the local market. The hiring manager in the global firm felt Tim's local knowledge would help their firm gain market share quickly, so they wooed him with a job offer as a team leader in payment technologies. Tim gladly accepted the offer.

In the new company, however, a problem surfaced in his team. One of Tim's team members, Ryan, a staff of three years, had always performed below par. This had not been an issue at first as Tim was trusted to lead and coach the team as he saw fit. But things came to a head when Tim received his first-ever negative peer appraisal, detailing how Tim had failed to collaborate with another team led by his peer. That full-paged, nasty, combative assessment brought a ton of scrutiny on Tim and his team. To make matters worse, Ryan made a major blunder around that same time which drew attention to his poor performance, reflecting badly on Tim.

For the first time in six years, Tim was labelled an 'ineffective leader', an ignominy he had never encountered in his successful career of 15 years. His ego and self-worth took a hit and that was when we began working together.

<u>Tim's goals</u>:
To meet the expectations of his superiors and
to manage his relationships with his team and his peers

Tim was a leader who had the heart to serve those whom he led. Under normal circumstances, this would have been a touching scenario. But in this case, the team had had enough. Tim was not able to support the rest of the group as he had spent the majority of his time working with Ryan.

Tim found it challenging to put Ryan on a performance management plan as Ryan was charming and kind. Tim believed the firm should be 'fair' to Ryan and give him another chance since he had tried his best.

The extra accommodations made for Ryan's poor performance seemed unfair to the rest. The balance had tipped and it was time to tip it back.

INDIVIDUALS vs TEAMS

In this paradox, leaders grapple with the contradiction between the needs of the individual and the needs of the team. In this regard, the idea of what is 'fair' or 'equal' come into play.

Is it fair to treat everyone the same way? Or since each person is different, shouldn't each one be treated differently, so we can be fair? This is a conundrum! Everyone wants 'fair' treatment but interprets 'fairness' differently.

This paradox occurs too when leaders need to make decisions concerning an individual in order to preserve the integrity and motivation of the team.

Leaders need to manage tension by focusing on individuals and teams appropriately and with 'fairness'.

TIM'S JOURNEY

THROUGH THE RE4 COACHING MODEL

STEP 1
RECONSTRUCT THE MAP

Tim became aware that he was spending too much time with one individual as he had become too personally invested. This took his attention away from other important areas.

STEP 2
REFRESH THE LENS

While Tim valued deep one-to-one relationships, his relationship with his stakeholders and responsibilities to his team were of a higher priority.

STEP 3
RENEW THE IDENTITY

Tim realized he needed to be more discerning. Actions he thought were helpful might be leading him downward instead. He needed to focus on higher priorities.

STEP 4
REBUILD THE CAPABILITIES

Tim committed to investing time to build relationships with his peer, his team and superiors, while still caring for the individual appropriately.

(Tim's comprehensive reflections can be found on pages 99 to 106.)

STEP 1: RECONSTRUCT THE MAP

Tim articulated his understanding of how individuals and teams interacted. He acknowledged that he had spent too much time on a single individual at the expense of his team.

Tim also realized he had taken on Ryan's performance as his personal responsibility and had become overly invested in helping Ryan. The conflict with his peer resulted from the stress of 'saving' Ryan. It was time to change his approach and reconsider his options.

STEP 2: REFRESH THE LENS

Tim saw that he was not making headway with his stakeholders and discerned that his leadership responsibilities to his entire team should take a higher priority. Regaining the trust of his superiors was also a non-negotiable. He became fiercely committed to finding productive ways to meet the developmental needs of all his team members, not only Ryan.

STEPS 3 & 4: RENEW THE IDENTITY & REBUILD THE CAPABILITIES

Tim used to see himself as someone who was bringing his team upwards. His new metaphor was the Penrose Steps, the optical illusion where one could seemingly climb forever and not get higher. It served as a reminder of his need to be discerning, as seemingly helpful actions might be leading him downward or in circles.

Tim committed to taking these actions:

1. Propose an intervention process for Ryan and seek endorsement from his superiors.
2. Conduct regular one-on-one meetings with each individual in the team and focus on their development.
3. Acknowledge his lapses and commit to supporting his team and peers better.

Tim's new narrative for success

Tim identified that one skill he needed before he could perform the actions was the ability to have authentic conversations. He wanted to acknowledge the lapse in how he discharged his duties and to commit to setting things right. So we devoted a session to role-play.

In one role-play scenario, he engaged his 'superiors' and shared his intervention plans in response to the feedback. In another, he practised speaking with his 'peer' and tried to repair the relationship.

After a couple of weeks, we met for our regular session. Tim had created the intervention plan for Ryan as agreed and had shared it with his superiors. He delivered the conversation in the way we had practised and was happy with the outcome. His superiors gave him valuable input and were appreciative that Tim was receptive to feedback. Tim's conversation with his peer, however, did not go as well. But Tim acknowledged that it would take time to rebuild trust. He actively followed up with requests for support from the other team and scheduled regular one-on-ones with his own team.

As for Ryan, it was too early to tell if the intervention would suffice. The improvements had been marginal. Tim and Ryan had arrived at the common understanding that Ryan's abilities might not be a good fit for his current role and that his development might be better served if he explored other avenues of work.

Tim recognized that while trying to help Ryan, he had become too involved and missed the forest for the tree. Taking an objective distance helped him to find a healthier way to approach issues. Tim created opportunities for others to support Ryan, allowing him to focus on his team and their developmental needs.

Tim regained his superiors' trust and found more effective ways to support all individuals in his team.

Systems citizenship starts with seeing the systems that we have shaped, which in turn shape us.

Peter M. Senge

PARADOX 3
SELF vs SYSTEM

AMY
A devoted in-house recruiter

"My spouse has been complaining about how much time I am spending on work," said Amy. "Although I work in a family-friendly organization where I am encouraged to knock-off on time, the truth is, I seem to be working 24/7, endlessly bound to my computer and mobile phone even when I am at home," she added.

When I first spoke with Amy, I was struck by her sense of responsibility toward her work. Like someone on a mission, she took her role as a recruiter very seriously. In her reckoning, her decision to hire or not to hire someone could potentially change their life. So, when she chose to not hire someone, she took care to break the news gently and coached the candidate to learn from the experience and improve his candidature for the future.

Professionally, she had earned the respect of her peers and established her credibility as a subject matter expert. Because she worked with a team that spanned a few time zones, Amy was always online. The ability to be responsive to her colleagues meant a lot to Amy. Her peers loved it, of course. However, tensions at home were high. Her spouse wished she would set her work aside more often and pull her weight at home. Unpleasant exchanges at home increased, pushing Amy to seek solace in her professional life where she felt affirmed, recognized and appreciated.

Over time, Amy's situation worsened. At work, she was troubled by conflicts at home, and after work, she was ridden with guilt, torn between her duty to work and her 'self' as a wife and mother.

<u>Amy's goals:</u>
To stop being overwhelmed by guilt and
perform well as a whole person

In the course of my work, I have come across countless executives like Amy whose careers defined them. The accolades, achievements and successes at work bolstered their self-esteem and became integral to their identity. The boundary between the professional identity and the private 'self' was eroded.

Amy's story resonated with me on a personal level as it reminded me of a season in my development. At that time, I was fully committed to my educational career, and as part of that system, I was a fully contributing individual. But my development took me to the point where that system no longer satisfied my aspirations. While I still enjoyed the work and the great camaraderie with colleagues, I felt it was time to leave. With great sadness and a tinge of hope, I finally took the plunge. It was a necessary step for my continued growth and professional development.

SELF vs SYSTEM

In this paradox, leaders struggle to keep their individual identity separate from the system in which they work.

The leader experiences tension between being self-focused and system-centric. The system feeds the identity of the leader, and conversely, the leader's personality and style also shape the identity of that system, and the lines between the 'self' and the 'system' are blurred.

The leader may feel pressured to conform to norms that compromise the sense of self and is troubled by these questions: should I lose myself so I can blend in? Or ignore others and just be me? How will I know if I am overly self-focused?

To achieve a state of balance in this paradox, the leader needs to regain a sense of 'self' and disentangle it from the 'system' while maintaining a healthy attachment.

AMY'S JOURNEY

THROUGH THE RE4 COACHING MODEL

STEP 1
RECONSTRUCT THE MAP

Amy realized she felt like a nobody without her job, though her family remained her top priority.

STEP 2
REFRESH THE LENS

Amy's relationship with her spouse and children were non-negotiable.

STEP 3
RENEW THE IDENTITY

Like a candle, Amy was limited in her capacity. She could only continue to shine when she replenished her 'self'.

STEP 4
REBUILD THE CAPABILITIES

Amy committed to establishing boundaries between her personal and professional life so she could perform better as a whole person.

(Amy's comprehensive reflections can be found on pages 109 to 116.)

STEP 1: RECONSTRUCT THE MAP

Amy was asked to sift through the identities that exist in her personal and professional life. She objectively concluded that she was living as if she was married to her job. She could not articulate a personal identity that existed outside of her work. The value she brought to her work and the appreciation of her colleagues informed her sense of self and self-worth. Without her work, she felt like a nobody. But when Amy examined her inner compass, she realized that her relationship with her family was most important to her core. She had focused so much on her role in the 'system' that she had neglected this aspect of her 'self'.

STEP 2: REFRESH THE LENS

Amy saw that she might have been avoiding her roles in her personal life as she did not want to feel like a failure. This, however, did not stop her guilt from piling up, because deep down, she greatly valued her family. She now saw the irony that while she was making a difference to others' lives, she was neglecting her children. It was time to take a new course of action to regain her 'self'.

STEPS 3 & 4: RENEW THE IDENTITY & REBUILD THE CAPABILITIES

Amy used to see herself as the sunlight that shone on everything, everywhere. She expended much energy trying to illuminate everything at work. When she took a fresh look at herself as a whole person, she adopted the metaphor of a candle. The candle reminded her that what she could give of herself was limited. Hence, she must conserve and replenish her 'self' so she could continue to shine and guide those with whom she interacted. Amy's most powerful shift was the recognition that she could continue to shine only when she replenished her 'self'. Only then could she have something to give.

Amy committed to taking these actions:

1. Establish boundaries between her professional and personal life.
2. Involve her spouse and discuss how she could meet both her professional and personal goals with his support.
3. Monitor and improve her physical energy, her focus and her emotions.

Amy's new narrative for success

Two weeks after we completed the coaching exercise, Amy looked much happier. She shared about her intention to be more available to her children and about the excellent conversations she had with her spouse.

Together, she and her spouse came up with a roster to share the responsibilities at home, allowing them more time with each other and the children. They also decided to outsource some housework so they could free up time to spend with the children.

Amy set some expectations for the occasions she had to work from home. Her spouse accepted that being prompt and responsive towards her team was vital to her and agreed to support her as much as he was able to. They set some boundaries on timings when she could work on weekends (for instance, when the children took their naps or had other scheduled activities). As a result of these limits they set, Amy became more disciplined and focused in her work.

Amy and her spouse determined to be good role models for their children and to always spend quality time as a family. They structured periods of time into their family routines where all of them would avoid using electronic devices. So much good resulted from their discussions!

To Amy, the metaphor of a candle served as a powerful reminder.

Every time she felt overwhelmed by guilt and anxiety that she was not responding quickly enough to the demands of work, she would remind herself that she needed to take time to replenish her 'self' so she could continue to shine. Her metaphor reminded her that her light, though limited, would still make a difference for someone. And that was enough.

Over time, Amy's anxiety lessened.
She was more productive at work and
happier with herself in both the personal
and professional arenas.

Amy learned to slow down and remind herself of why she was doing what she was doing and how she was going about it. When the demands on her pressed in, she took a clear look within and responded according to her inner compass. She now functioned well within the 'system' without compromising her 'self'.

Leading and following
are complementary
actions like inhaling
and exhaling.
They are both essential
in leadership.

PARADOX 4
LEADING vs FOLLOWING

CHRISTOPHER
A technical leader heading a team of SMEs

My first conversation with Christopher left a deep impression. A senior director in a large internet software company, Christopher took our call while in transit at an airport, so we could only connect via a phone call without video.

But through his voice, I sensed despair. He had just emerged from another technical discussion with one of his team members. He sounded deflated. That conversation, like many others before, riddled him with self-doubt as he was unable to fully comprehend the intricacies of newer technologies as quickly as his younger team members, many of whom were digital natives. As a result of that feeling of inadequacy, Christopher was torn between stepping back and letting someone else take the reins, or investing a ludicrous amount of time to acquire the technical know-how so he could code as well as his team could.

When I asked him to rate his effectiveness as a leader of his team, he surprised me with a score of six out of ten. To be honest, I was not expecting that, given that the picture he had just painted was so bleak. Asked to justify the score, he clearly articulated his strengths — he could provide wisdom and direction for projects given his years of experience; he could ensure his team received the support and resources they needed to succeed while doing what they enjoyed.

<u>*Christopher's goals*</u>*:*
To stay motivated in his role,
find creative ways to lead and contribute,
and raise his leadership influence

To help frame our work together, I asked Christopher to describe the traits of a good leader. He replied, "Only the best member of the team is worthy of being the leader of that group."

Christopher felt that a leader should be the best individual contributor as well as an inspiring leader. It's small wonder that he was beating himself up — he was not succeeding as an individual contributor since he had a merely conceptual grasp of the new technologies his team was working with.

Being in a role where age and technical knowledge seemed to be inversely proportional, Christopher's definition of leadership and his expectations of himself sapped his enthusiasm and motivation, extinguishing any hopes of success.

LEADING vs FOLLOWING

Most individual contributors rise to become leaders through their initiative and natural leadership ability. Excellent learners, they become subject matter experts early in their careers, distinguish themselves as 'having the best brains' and earn respect and support despite having no official title as a leader. They usually wield soft power — the ability to influence.

These people prove themselves over time, rise through the ranks and are given the reins over large portfolios. Many who find themselves in this position usually see a need for additional support through coaching.

In Industry 4.0, the threat of becoming obsolete is more real than ever before. A few of my clients have lamented that age is their natural disadvantage. Their confidence takes another hit when the more they learn, the more they realize how little they actually know. This is a paradox of learning — when the sum of what you know appears microscopically small when you become aware of the mass of information out there.

Here is a truth that may sound strange. To rise from being a follower to a leader, you have to lead. To experience success as a leader, you need to unlearn what you have learned. You need to expand your inventory of skills and not rely only on methods that brought you to this point.

CHRISTOPHER'S JOURNEY
THROUGH THE RE4 COACHING MODEL

STEP 1
RECONSTRUCT THE MAP

Christopher's main issue was trying to be the 'best' member of his team. His team did have good things going for it.

STEP 2
REFRESH THE LENS

Christopher realized he could not possibly know everything. It was time to get creative in finding other ways to contribute.

STEP 3
RENEW THE IDENTITY

Like every tool in a toolbox, everyone has a unique role and value. He was complemented by his team.

STEP 4
REBUILD THE CAPABILITIES

Christopher committed to be authentic and risk being vulnerable with his team. He would communicate how each person, including himself, could contribute to the team vision.

(Christopher's comprehensive reflections can be found on pages 119 to 126.)

STEP 1: RECONSTRUCT THE MAP

Christopher was asked to objectively list the value each member of the team (including himself) brought. We spent time identifying what was going well. This left him with an insight that despite things not going as smoothly as he had desired, the reality was not as bad as he had perceived it to be. His self-deprecating side was getting the better of him. He also recognized that part of the issue was his desire to be 'the best' in the team, which hindered him from learning and growing in his role as a leader.

STEP 2: REFRESH THE LENS

As we discussed a paradox of 'knowing enough' versus 'we will never know enough', Christopher learned that the goal he had set for himself was humanly unattainable. Instead of fixating on that, he could find other ways to contribute. He also needed to work on being authentic and vulnerable, while still feeling worthy to lead.

STEPS 3 & 4: RENEW THE IDENTITY & REBUILD THE CAPABILITIES

Christopher used to see himself as a Swiss army knife who could 'do it all' without help from others. As he reviewed his contribution objectively, he saw that he added value to the team by his experience and strategic focus. His new metaphor was to be one of the tools in a toolbox, complemented by other tools (his team members). As a leader, he could provide the platform for each of his crew to showcase their strengths. The most powerful shift for Christopher was to recognize that he did not have to be the impenetrable 'do-it-all' and 'know-it-all' but should instead build a strong, cohesive team of leaders.

Christopher committed to taking these actions:

1. Seek alignment with his team on their expectations of him and what he could contribute in terms of strategic focus.
2. Communicate authentically on how they could support one another.
3. Create a compelling team vision, clear strategic direction and career development opportunities for each team member.
4. Complete a gratitude exercise daily to acknowledge his contribution and achievement.

Christopher's new narrative for success

The strides Christopher made after our sessions went beyond my expectations and blew me away. Our first session had felt so gloomy and heavy, I left wondering if he could pull himself through.

The next meeting two weeks later could not have been more different — it was so full of hope! As we examined the paradox and his original notion of leadership in our second session, I felt as if I was speaking to a different person.

As Christopher started looking at ways in which he could bring unique value, the support from his team boosted his confidence even further. At the end of our coaching engagement,

Christopher became more authentic, and comfortable in showing vulnerability. He stopped expecting himself to be impenetrable or to know everything.

He also accepted that rallying strong support from his team was going to be a long process, and that different ones would come on board at different times. He respectfully gave each person time and reached out consistently, which increased his credibility.

Once he had let go of the need to be the Swiss army knife, his sense of security increased. He felt it was reasonable to ask for help and found his team more than happy to offer their expert opinions. He used those opportunities to showcase and acknowledge the talents in his team. Needless to say, this boosted team morale.

Over the next four months, Christopher's confidence in his leadership ability grew leaps and bounds. While still pushing himself to understand trends in the industry, his motivation was now not about 'catching up' but about learning enough so he could lead by providing insight and strategic direction.

As he embraced his love for his technical field, his personal life turned around as well. Life became lighter. Instead of being withdrawn and defeated, he was more self-compassionate and able to connect with his family.

*He could now laugh at his shortcomings
and handle things with a sense of humor.*

Months later, Christopher's efforts were validated when he received startlingly high praise for his leadership and influence from his staff in an employee satisfaction survey. A few of them said he had become their ideal role model. It was a vast difference from the discouraging feedback he had received before.

*He was greatly encouraged and found
renewed motivation in his leadership role.*

An organization's
reason for being,
like that of any organism,
is to help the parts
that are in relationship
to each other, to be able
to deal with change
in the environment.

Kevin Kelly

PARADOX 5
BOTTOM-UP vs TOP-DOWN

ADELINE
A change agent in a large traditional enterprise

Adeline and I had worked together some years ago. She was, in fact, an agile coach herself. We reconnected when she sought my professional help for a situation she was facing. (Some of my clients are agile coaches and scrum masters involved in enterprise transformation.)

At the time, Adeline had been hired to spearhead changes in one of the largest private companies in Asia. The senior management of that organization had heard about agility and was intrigued by its potential benefits. They hired Adeline to coach the organization exclusively for two years.

Now, if you have been involved in enterprise transformations, you would know how stressful these seasons of massive changes can be. Adeline's company was no different. It was an organization with a long tradition and many entrenched processes. Change, already a challenging process, was made more so by the sheer size of this organization. The management, not wanting to rock the boat too much, gave Adeline the target to bring agile practices into 20 percent of the organization within a year.

When we spoke, I could see that Adeline was feeling pressured that her efforts in this organization were not meeting with progress at the rate she had hoped to see. She had been trying to work from all angles, sometimes helping teams to see the benefits of agile methodologies, habits and rituals, other times dialoguing with senior management to rally support for systemic changes.

"What I love most, Chuen Chuen, is working with the teams," she confided. "I have such satisfaction seeing their eyes suddenly light up when they understand how the new way of working can transform their world!" she enthused like a true-blue agile coach. Unfortunately, the middle managers had adopted a 'wait and see' attitude, preferring to stay in the safety of the status quo. Dialogues with senior management usually left her frustrated as their conversations centred around her lack of tangible results.

Adeline's goals:
To increase the impact of the transformation and speed
up the pace of change with greater economy of effort

We made excellent progress during our first session. Being a coach herself, Adeline quickly identified possible actions that could increase her effectiveness in bringing transformation. But she also saw the misalignment between the teams on the ground, the middle management and the senior management. She had been trying to get buy-in from the management and drive change from the ground-up by helping teams achieve better results. However, she was limited in her capacity as a 'Lone Ranger', trying to spin this very heavy wheel of change. Though she loved her job and believed in her mission, she knew she could easily burn out before even half her work was done if she carried on that way.

Adeline understood what she was up against. Changing mindsets was the key to lasting transformation and she knew she could not do it alone. She needed allies at different levels of the organization in order to reach her goals.

BOTTOM-UP vs TOP-DOWN

A top-down approach is, traditionally, one where direction is given and methods for its implementation are cascaded down from global headquarters, the 'seat of power'.

Top-down initiatives can at times be effective or even necessary. For instance, when the management needs to implement an unpopular initiative which can bring long-term gains that outweigh any short-term pain. Once a decision is made at the top level of leadership, instructions are disseminated to regional offices, where changes quickly take effect.

I have seen examples where top-down initiatives failed. I am sure you have too. Can you recall, for instance, a time when an announcement from headquarters left staff perturbed at how the decision was made and implemented? They might have felt angered that decisions and processes which directly impacted them were implemented without adequate warning or prior consultation.

Does this mean we should sway completely to the bottom-up approach, listen to the people on the ground or do what the majority wants?

When a leader leans too much to the top-down management style, he may find himself fighting with the people who are supposed to execute the plans. If he leans too much to the bottom-up approach, he might be paralyzed by indecision, caught between camps of opposing ideas. The paradox of top-down versus bottom-up describes this tension.

Whichever the dominant or preferred leadership style, a leader should examine his or her approach when faced with fierce resistance or stalled plans.

ADELINE'S JOURNEY

THROUGH THE RE4 COACHING MODEL

STEP 1
RECONSTRUCT THE MAP

Driving change purely through the bottom-up approach was going to take too much time and effort.

STEP 2
REFRESH THE LENS

Adeline did not have to influence everyone on her own — she had partners she could work with to create both a top-down and a bottom-up influence.

STEP 3
RENEW THE IDENTITY

Adeline needed to create a series of network repeaters to broadcast her signal and influence without losing its strength.

STEP 4
REBUILD THE CAPABILITIES

Adeline committed to increasing her influence through others.

(Adeline's comprehensive reflections can be found on pages 129 to 136.)

STEP 1: RECONSTRUCT THE MAP

Adeline saw how futile it had been to lean heavily on driving change through the bottom-up approach. Though she experienced promising moments where she was able to influence teams to make significant changes, it still felt as if she was swimming against the tide. It would take a long time to reach her goals and she was in danger of burning out. Support from the senior management depended on whether she could create more tangible, quantifiable results.

STEP 2: REFRESH THE LENS

Adeline could see she was spreading herself too thin, trying to 'change the world' single-handedly. Her burden could be lightened if she worked with middle managers who could provide top-down support for teams and bottom-up influence for senior management.

STEPS 3 & 4: RENEW THE IDENTITY & REBUILD THE CAPABILITIES

Adeline's metaphor for her previous state was a spider web — spread too thin to be of use. Her new metaphor was a series of network repeaters which reminded her of the need to co-opt others to help broadcast her signal and influence without losing its strength.

Adeline committed to taking these actions:

1. Set up a task force consisting of supportive and influential middle managers, so together, they could create a wider impact.
2. Look into training promising scrum masters so teams could be better supported.
3. Spend her time more strategically (that is, with teams that could produce the most significant impact).

Adeline's new narrative for success

A few weeks later, Adeline came to our next session with renewed excitement and gusto.

She had successfully formed a task force with four other middle managers who were already intrigued and inspired by the possibilities of being agile. Her discussions with them spotlighted other opportunities she had not thought of before and gave her new perspective.

> *Feeling much less alone, Adeline was*
> *more purposeful and confident that*
> *she could achieve the target.*

With the involvement of the four managers, the excitement among the teams grew and spread as more became curious about exploring ways to do things differently.

Adeline had successfully implemented one characteristic of agile teams — empowerment. She was one step closer to her goal of working with greater economy of effort.

While she understood that bringing transformation in such a large organization was going to take time, Adeline was confident her new approach was going to be more effective and enjoyable than her earlier one.

Two ways to influence
human behavior;
you can manipulate it
or you can inspire it.

Simon Sinek

PARADOX 6
EXECUTING vs INSPIRING

PRAKASH
A technical leader and advisor to top-level management

Prakash struck me as being one of the most soft-spoken clients I had ever worked with. A technical expert, he had risen through the ranks, accumulating experience, earning the trust and respect from colleagues and leaders alike. He now fielded an interesting role in a financial technology company in Europe as a trusted technical advisor to many C-level leaders, with a 'dotted-line relationship' to various heads of departments.

With his calm demeanor, Prakash appeared very unassuming and was easy to connect with. I could imagine why teams might see him as a brotherly figure and enjoy working with him.

Analytical and organized, Prakash came to our first session well-prepared with facts. He shared his conundrum: with the emergence of data analytics, he saw an opportunity to use data mined from customer-service to feed into the product design cycle to improve product design and customer satisfaction.

"This can potentially change the future of the company and enable us to be pre-emptive instead of reactive," he enthused. Excited, he had set some key performance indicators and shared them with the team. He was surprised, however, by the strong pushback from them.

<u>Prakash's goals:</u>
To increase his ability to influence and
inspire the team to make a difficult but strategic change

A short while into our coaching, Prakash began to see a pattern in his interactions with the team. He realized that though they were tight-knit and team members approached him readily for help, he had not been able to push them to perform at their full potential. The team resisted him as his plans required a massive amount of work, especially at the initial stages; they saw only the added sweat but not the fruit that would result.

Prakash was understandably annoyed at what he perceived to be their stubbornness and resistance to change. He was frustrated because he knew they were capable of more but could not help them perform at their highest potential. Being nurturing had not worked, but he did not want to switch to a forceful approach as it was simply not his style. Not being their direct manager made it an even greater challenge to motivate them.

To reach his goals, Prakash had to work on two fronts — how he perceived himself and how he was engaging others.

EXECUTING vs INSPIRING

In this paradox, leaders are so focused on completing a task they forget to inspire the people with whom they work. To resolve this paradox, two aspects must be balanced:

1. Help employees understand the reasons that make the effort worthwhile, the 'why' of the task (Sinek, 2009). This is the 'fuel' that motivates people to push through challenges.

2. Set them up for success by equipping them with the right skills and tools, such as good judgment, discernment and problem-solving skills. Inspiration alone is not enough. An understanding of the objectives will ensure sound decisions can be made, even in the absence of the leader.

Let us look at each of these aspects in turn.

Firstly, research shows that employees want to find meaning in work. When an organization helps its workers see the value of their work, it reaps positive effects ranging from talent retention and higher engagement to profitability. I often share with clients that most people do not mind working hard, but they mind doing work that seems meaningless. Leaders should regularly communicate:

- Why a project was put in place
- Where the employees fit in the overall plan
- How their success contributes to the organization's vision

Secondly, employees need the right skills and tools. Leaders should consider:

- How to teach employees to think in the face of constraints
- How to teach employees to weigh options according to organizational goals
- What tools are at their disposal and what skills they can be developed in

By equipping employees with appropriate advanced cognitive abilities and soft skills, leaders can raise competency, cultivate the next line of leaders in the organization and leave a legacy.

PRAKASH'S JOURNEY

THROUGH THE RE4 COACHING MODEL

STEP 1
RECONSTRUCT THE MAP

Prakash was the only one who could see the benefits of the initiative while the team had a different perspective.

STEP 2
REFRESH THE LENS

For his idea to take off, Prakash needed the team to understand the benefits and commit to the vision.

STEP 3
RENEW THE IDENTITY

A conductor leads the orchestra, but the musicians are the ones who make the music.

STEP 4
REBUILD THE CAPABILITIES

Prakash committed to facilitating cooperative brainstorming and decision-making instead of simply instructing.

(Prakash's comprehensive reflections can be found on pages 139 to 146.)

STEP 1: RECONSTRUCT THE MAP

Prakash firmly believed that the changes he was proposing, albeit difficult for the initial months, would ultimately benefit employees and the company. His reasons were compelling. However, he reflected that the team might have seen only the additional work and not the reasons behind his plans. This eased his frustration toward their initial reactions and helped him empathize with them more.

STEP 2: REFRESH THE LENS

Prakash saw that he had taken on sole responsibility for achieving the vision. He recognized that he needed to get buy-in from the team and inspire intrinsic motivation within the entire team.

STEPS 3 & 4: RENEW THE IDENTITY & REBUILD THE CAPABILITIES

Prakash pictured his previous state as a person dragging an unwilling horse to a watering hole — forcing something good on someone without his willing participation. His new metaphor was that of an orchestra where he was the conductor and team members were the musicians. Just as a conductor cannot make music without the musicians, he could not accomplish his goals without his team's full and willing participation.

Prakash committed to taking these actions:

1. Compellingly pitch his vision, explaining why it was important.
2. Facilitate brainstorming and let the team come up with solutions to actualize new ways of designing products.
3. Let his team take the lead in final decisions.

Prakash's new narrative for success

Prakash wanted to learn how he could develop critical thinking in his team. For this, I introduced him to Richard Paul's 'Wheel of Reasoning' (Paul & Binker, 1990). Over two coaching sessions, we worked through the eight sectors of the wheel. Prakash applied this learning to guide discussions without dictating the team's direction.

The discussions became more effective
and drew greater involvement
from the team.

He had satisfied the inspiration aspect. Now, he could step back as conversations within the team gained momentum and they began to imagine a better future together. They debated the best way to use data collected from customers to feed the design process and create better products. They tackled issues at the root and improved client satisfaction. Prakash had successfully applied the reasoning framework to unite the team behind the vision and to help them learn to make decisions aligned to their goals.

When we met again two weeks later, Prakash was beaming from ear to ear.

Prakash had gotten full buy-in from the team.

Once everyone took ownership of the vision, he no longer had to drag them along. Motivation skyrocketed and the team birthed many new ideas when he successfully inspired them and equipped them with the right thinking tools.

Leaders need a wide
repertoire of approaches
to attain their goals –
to be hot as steam,
cool as ice,
or fluid as water
as circumstances require.

PARADOX 7
ENFORCING vs EMPOWERING

BENG CHUAN
A senior director with a boss who micro-managed

Beng Chuan impressed me from the start. I was blown away by his eloquence, his emotional intelligence and his quick rise to the position of senior director despite his relatively young age (he was then under 40). When he recounted some of the most difficult conversations he had had with his bosses, I envied his courage and secretly wished I had been like him at that age.

Tough conversations, it seemed, were nothing new to Beng Chuan. He knew how to present his case clearly, with the right tone and with choice facts. I was not surprised, therefore, to learn that he had been identified as next-in-line for a C-level leadership position, way ahead of most of my clients his age.

Beng Chuan needed coaching through a challenging period of transition. He had just gotten a new boss who exercised a style of leadership that clashed with his. Beng Chuan was empowering and delegated readily. But this new manager over him preferred to be in full control and was extremely fastidious.

Beng Chuan's manager would pass complex work directly to his team without clear instructions, usually near the end of the day, and would expect the work to be completed the following morning. Beng Chuan found out that some of his team, not daring to object to his manager, had worked till past midnight on many nights, but were still unable to clear the ever-increasing workload.

As his manager had bypassed him entirely, Beng Chuan had no clear sight of his team's workload, and did not know the rationale behind the work his team was assigned. Beng Chuan found himself sandwiched as he would hear the team's grouses, as well as his manager's dissatisfaction about his team's inefficiency and missed deadlines. He was unable to defend either side as he struggled to agree with his manager's leadership style. He was, however, not eager to take the matter up with his manager as they were relatively new to each other and Beng Chuan did not want to add stress on their relationship.

<u>Beng Chuan's goals</u>:
To empower his team and his new manager,
help both parties succeed and
gain the trust of his manager

The case Beng Chuan presented was more complex than the usual cases of 'Enforcing versus Empowering' as it involved 'managing up'. It required Beng Chuan to leverage his tact and emotional intelligence to negotiate with his manager.

ENFORCING vs EMPOWERING

This paradox is about the leadership approach — how much control to give and how assertive the leader should be.

Most people prefer to be empowered as empowerment is usually associated with trust and autonomy (Pink, 2009). Someone who feels empowered may say things like: "My boss trusts me to make the best decisions and gives me full autonomy to do my work in the way I think best." Or they may say, "I am allowed to be creative and resourceful. And when I am stuck, I can turn to my boss for support and guidance." Empowerment of staff is also positively associated with improved morale and commitment.

Does this mean all leaders should be empowering?

While this has been advocated as a preferred leadership style, a leader might need to be more enforcing and prescriptive in some situations, such as when employees lack the maturity or readiness to take greater responsibility, or where protocols or standards must be strictly followed.

To navigate this paradox, a leader must recognize that different circumstances require different leadership styles.

BENG CHUAN'S JOURNEY
THROUGH THE RE4 COACHING MODEL

STEP 1
RECONSTRUCT THE MAP

The way Beng Chuan had dealt with the situation was not helpful to all parties.

STEP 2
REFRESH THE LENS

Clear boundaries were needed between Beng Chuan and his manager.

STEP 3
RENEW THE IDENTITY

Just as a bee and flowers exist in a symbiotic relationship, Beng Chuan and his manager needed each other while functioning in their separate roles.

STEP 4
REBUILD THE CAPABILITIES

Beng Chuan committed to having the tough conversation with his manager and meeting the needs of all parties.

(Beng Chuan's comprehensive reflections can be found on pages 149 to 156.)

STEP 1: RECONSTRUCT THE MAP

Beng Chuan courageously acknowledged that the way he had been dealing with the situation was not empowering for his team. The lack of trust and open communication between him and his manager had created a negative work culture where his team was overworked and under-appreciated.

STEP 2: REFRESH THE LENS

While being respected by his manager was vital to Beng Chuan, he saw that his lack of action had encouraged his manager's behavior. He also recognized that he wanted to be seen as an empowering leader by his team, someone who helped them succeed. He knew he had to create clear boundaries between him and his manager.

STEPS 3 & 4: RENEW THE IDENTITY & REBUILD THE CAPABILITIES

Beng Chuan described his previous state as a soldier who followed orders; he fully complied with his manager. His new metaphor was a bee, which has a symbiotic relationship with flowers as a pollinator. Through this metaphor, Beng Chuan framed his relationship with his manager as a symbiotic one where neither could do without the other and each had a part to play in a mutually beneficial relationship. To empower his team, Beng Chuan needed to enforce boundaries with his manager.

Beng Chuan committed to taking these actions:

1. Deliver honest feedback to his manager respectfully to help him see the impact of his actions on the team.

2. Make assertive requests on the way of working between them, while making room for his manager's need for control.

Beng Chuan's new narrative for success

Beng Chuan and I connected some weeks later and he seemed to be hugely relieved. I knew something had happened and waited for him to share.

Heaving a sigh, Beng Chuan announced that he had the dreaded 'confrontation' with his manager.

Since he had expected a defensive response, he picked the best moment to broach the topic. To prepare for the meeting, he had sent an email to set the context and state his intentions. Beng Chuan had framed the context as a problem they both were facing — the efficiency of the team. He shared that he had some ideas in mind and wanted to brainstorm them with his manager before he made any decision. The email got his manager's attention.

They had the conversation a few days later.

Instead of receiving defensive and curt replies, Beng Chuan found his manager approachable and interested in tackling the issue together. Beng Chuan objectively presented his side of the story describing the issues he faced:

1. He did not have an overview of the team's workload as the work was delegated to them without his knowledge. He acknowledged that this was an unintended consequence of work needing urgently to be distributed. Unfortunately, this resulted in him not being able to support his team as effectively as he would have liked.

2. The team did not challenge the authority of his manager out of respect, but this respect, taken to an extreme, resulted in reduced transparency and honesty — another unintended consequence. They were overloaded with work as a result.

    Beng Chuan noted that his manager listened and took the

message well as no blame was attributed and all observations were objective. Beng Chuan then proposed that he should be the intermediary for information exchange between his team and his manager, as that would yield the following advantages:

1. His manager would be free to focus on the big picture and more pressing matters.
2. The team would be better able to meet deadlines as Beng Chuan would manage the allocation of resources according to priorities.
3. Beng Chuan would resolve challenges within his team and escalate only cases that required his manager's attention.

Beng Chuan satisfied his manager's need for control by offering to give weekly progress updates, without the presence of the team. This would free the team from having to sit through meetings listening to updates that were irrelevant to them.

Beng Chuan successfully created a structure for information flow that satisfied both his manager and his team and empowered each party to thrive in their roles with his support.

At the end of our engagement,

Beng Chuan gained his manager's trust,
established clear boundaries between them,
and empowered both his manager
and his team to succeed.

Learn to know yourself…
to search realistically and
regularly the processes
of your own mind
and feelings.

Nelson Mandela

PARADOX 8
PRINCIPLED vs ADAPTABLE

KELLY
A millennial people-leader considering next steps

"My work is so boring," Kelly said flatly. "I am doing the same old thing every day."

A high-flyer who blazed a trail to the top a few years after leaving school, Kelly and I were engaged in a chemistry call where we explored her greatest challenges and what she wanted to resolve through our coaching. "I want meaning and purpose in my career, but I am going in circles. I feel stuck. Perhaps I should move on, but this is not the right time," she replied.

Kelly had become a people-leader in under three years of starting work and was frequently headhunted after her meteoric rise. Change had been her only constant as she craved excitement, new challenges and opportunities to learn skills. One of her favourite phrases was: "If you ain't growing, you ain't living".

Now eight years into her career, Kelly had just started a family and was reconsidering the options in this phase of life. She briefly shared her explorations with me, but it seemed that all the possibilities circled back to the same conclusion — it didn't seem a good time to move. The available options were not as attractive as her current position and could not compete with the benefits and compensation she was enjoying.

"Perhaps, it's a season to stay safe and go slower," she said pensively, still unsure of her decision.

Kelly decided to work with me more intensively to get over this rut and find renewed meaning and purpose in her career.

Kelly's goals:
To explore ways to create meaning and
find renewed purpose in her career

Over our next two sessions, Kelly and I explored aspects of her roles and discussed what she found meaningful. She was a great fit for her job and had just the right profile — great people skills, analytical and strategic thinking, great story-telling ability and persuasiveness. And yet, Kelly's dissatisfaction had grown over time until the only reason for her to remain in her job seemed to be the salary.

Kelly's story reminded me of a season in my career. I have been called a 'stick-in-the-mud' once or twice, partly in jest. But there's no smoke without fire. I am thankful for friends in the workplace who shared their honest opinion of me. They helped me reflect on my behavior — had I been too rigidly fixated on principles, values and beliefs? And was it time to adapt and refine those values?

Now, it was Kelly's turn to find the answers for herself. The coaching exercise she was about to embark on was going to help her achieve a significant shift in her mindset to remain true to her principles and find fulfilment in her career.

PRINCIPLED vs ADAPTABLE

This paradox describes the need for leaders to stay true to their principles, their 'true north' and yet remain adaptable.

To resolve this paradox, the leader needs to know when to remain unchanged and when to adapt. In this volatile world, the best decision is often not immediately apparent.

But one thing is clear. Leaders must be decisive about whether to maintain the status quo or to adapt and evolve. Either way, a clear choice must be made, so the resultant actions flow from a commitment to a plan and not from indecisiveness or inaction.

Leaders face this paradox under various scenarios such as changes in leadership, team structure or personal life. I have had clients who underwent trying circumstances that mired them in this paradox — one experienced six changes of leadership within seven years; another faced severe attrition within the team, and yet another experienced multiple restructuring in the organization. To navigate seasons like these, leaders need to know whether to stay constant or adapt and change.

KELLY'S JOURNEY

THROUGH THE RE4 COACHING MODEL

STEP 1
RECONSTRUCT THE MAP

Kelly realized that her successes were a result of
her personality and drive, and that her career
still had much that was positive.

STEP 2
REFRESH THE LENS

She identified other areas of growth
while remaining in the same role.

STEP 3
RENEW THE IDENTITY

Like a rain tree with an overgrown branch,
Kelly's growth needed to even out
holistically.

STEP 4
REBUILD THE CAPABILITIES

Kelly committed to identifying other ways
to define growth and to focus on aspects
of her life apart from her career.

(Kelly's comprehensive reflections can be found on pages 159 to 166.)

STEP 1: RECONSTRUCT THE MAP

Kelly was aware of her drive for achievement. Her successes thus far had been due to her personality and drive. While she felt that things could always be improved upon, there was no real reason for her discontentment as her career still offered a lot that was positive.

STEP 2: REFRESH THE LENS

Kelly remained true to her value of being a strong contributor at work. She had a strong sense of loyalty and gratitude to those who mentored her. She elevated her definition of professionalism and began to see other ways in which she could grow while remaining in the same role.

Kelly also examined how she was living her life as a whole and refocused on relationships with her family.

STEPS 3 & 4: RENEW THE IDENTITY & REBUILD THE CAPABILITIES

Kelly described her previous state as a lush rain tree with an off-balanced, overgrown branch. Her new metaphor was of a healthy rain tree with evenly-developed branches. It represented her desire to grow holistically and intentionally.

Kelly committed to taking these actions:

1. Redefine what growth could look like in her current role.
2. Bring her parents on a trip, which, in her reckoning, was four years overdue.

Kelly's new narrative for success

A few weeks later, Kelly and I reconnected for our regular session. She gushed excitedly about the newfound 'gems' in her work.

"I found at least three projects I could learn and grow in. It's taking my work to the next level!" she said. "I spoke to my superior and my team and they are even more excited than I was! This showed me that the opportunities to stretch and grow had been there all along if only I knew where to look," she said.

Kelly had created a map of the branches of her life. Using the metaphor of the rain tree, Kelly identified areas in which she had to grow so the foliage would be balanced and equally lush. She remained true to her principles while adapting how she lived them.

When I asked her to measure her sense of meaning and purpose in her career, she paused and reflected.

"Outwardly, nothing has changed. I am in the same role and designation, working with the same team and stakeholders. My scope has not increased. Yet today, when I think about your question, I feel that my work is twice as meaningful and purposeful than it had been. It's amazing how I still have the same principles but adapting the way I choose to live has led to such a different outcome. My focus has shifted from a micro-level view of my career to a macro view of my entire life," she said, her eyes sparkling. "I am now able to zoom out from looking at growth in the next two to three years of my career to looking at the next eight to ten years of my life. This perspective gave me insights into how I need to evolve my principles as I progress into a different stage of life," Kelly said.

At the end of our coaching engagement,

> *Kelly's work felt more meaningful*
> *and purposeful than it had before.*

Kelly discovered an important truth — an internal shift of mindset is often more essential than an external change in circumstances. The 'DNA' of our mindset, values, beliefs and principles determine our behavior and our external realities — and hence the outcomes.

PART III

TAKING THINGS FORWARD

CLOSING THOUGHTS

The world is changing inexorably. To resist change is futile.

As leaders, we need to evolve and level-up constantly. To learn, unlearn, relearn rapidly. We need to see what others cannot yet see, anticipate what others do not yet anticipate, and identify challenges that can threaten the existence of our businesses and organizations.

In this rapidly changing world, knowledge quickly becomes obsolete. Leadership beliefs, too, must be quickly updated and replaced. Leaders can lead with greater agility by keeping three fundamentals in mind:

1. Know your authentic self — your values and inner compass.
2. Be sensitive to stress — it signals that a paradox is present and changes are required.
3. Finding the answer right for your context is far more important than finding the 'right' answer.

The process of becoming agile begins with creating a mental image of the desired outcome. Consider what needs to be challenged and explore how to shift your mindset — your greatest asset — to bring about the change.

You can apply the Re4 Coaching Model as a structured approach to support you through a mindset shift. Once that happens, take massive action. Experiment. Review. Try again. Fly the plane as you build it. The journey is going to be exciting. The process of finding answers to manage paradoxes is not easy, but it is precisely what you need to develop true agility, so you can lead and inspire in the real world.

RE4 COACHING MODEL EXERCISES

In the following pages, you will find this treasure trove of resources:

- Comprehensive reflections of the individuals portrayed in Part II of this book. They serve as examples of how to apply the Re4 Coaching Model.

- Re4 Coaching Model Exercises — for your own reflections as you work through the Re4 Coaching Model. (Printable PDF templates of these exercises can be downloaded at ***ACESENCE.com/Re4-exercises***. Simply scan the QR code on the next page to access them.)

How the exercises are structured

For each paradox, there are four steps to work through:

STEP 1: RECONSTRUCT THE MAP

STEP 2: REFRESH THE LENS

STEP 3: RENEW THE IDENTITY

STEP 4: REBUILD THE CAPABILITIES

Questions are provided at each step to help you achieve the objectives specific to that step.

Questions in Step 1 differ in each paradox, to draw out what is different in each context. Questions in Steps 2 to 4 are identical for all the paradoxes. Depending on your context, you may find some questions more pertinent than others. Feel free to substitute words or rephrase questions to make them more relevant.

Working on your own

Give yourself at least 30 minutes of undisturbed time to work through the exercises for each paradox.

Read the questions and freely write what comes to mind without self-censorship. To navigate each paradox, define the circumstances in your own words and establish measures of success.

Revisit your reflections at least twice, giving yourself time between each session, as new perspectives can take time to surface and become clear.

As you work through the exercises, you will understand your perspectives better as you examine the conflict of priorities between two opposite ends of the paradox. You will also be better able to articulate the relationship between them. If you are unsure about how to do the exercises, refer to the examples on their facing pages.

Working with a coach

You can also work with a coach who may offer alternative questions to help you clarify your perspective and your stand.

To prepare for a personalized leadership development with a professional coach, you can use the Leadership Agility Evaluation Checklist at *ACESENCE.com/Agility-checklist* (or scan the QR code on page 178). This assessment will identify your strengths in leadership agility and areas in which you can improve.

To explore the possibility of engaging my services as a coach, please see pages 170-171. I will be pleased to connect with you.

 Scan this QR code to access printable PDF templates of the Re4 Coaching Model Exercises at *ACESENCE.com/Re4-exercises*

TASKS vs PEOPLE

SERENE

PROFILE

- A high performer in a global technology company.
- Worked in a multinational team with a manager and three teammates in regional offices within different time zones.
- A go-getter and eyes-on-the-ball type of leader.
- Seen as someone who could be counted on to deliver results on time and on target.
- Meeting targets at work fed her self-worth.

CHALLENGE

Received negative feedback through a 360 assessment exercise.

GOALS

To develop her career, see growth in scope and an increase in responsibilities.

See how Serene navigated the paradox using the Re4 Coaching Model.

SERENE'S REFLECTIONS

STEP 1: RECONSTRUCT THE MAP

A. Which is more important to you most often, tasks or people?

At work, I am goal-driven and task-focused. I will take no nonsense. Finishing tasks at speed is important. No one dares mess with my deadlines, or they will get it from me. I guess I really should not be surprised by the 360 feedback.

B. Under what circumstances does your preference change? Why?

My preference shifts when I am not leading a project. I respect authority, so I let the project lead set the pace. This is true with my boss as well — I often give in to him. I care too much about my career to antagonize him.

   At home, I am completely different — more people-oriented. My family means everything to me. I protect my time with them fiercely. Perhaps this is why I have to complete work promptly, so I do not need to put in extra hours!

C. On a scale of 1 to 10 (*1 being worst and 10 being best*), how effective is your approach? What are your thoughts on your score?

I place my effectiveness with people at a 5. I wouldn't say things are going poorly at work, but it seems unlikely that I will progress further. I've a good number of accomplishments and I'm known for doing things promptly. But my 360 assessment paints a different picture. I didn't enjoy reading those comments. I feel misunderstood. They didn't see the positive side of my strictness about deadlines.

   Things at home are going well. No complaints. I don't mind working irregular hours due to time zones. The flexible work hours sometimes gives me pockets of free time in the middle of the day.

D. What needs to happen to increase the score?

I must improve my relationships. The 360 assessment showed that my global teammates found me unfriendly. I recall times when I snapped at colleagues who asked how my weekend was. I also recall a conflict with a colleague in marketing. She had requested on Friday evening for me to prepare a report by Monday morning. I firmly declined as I was unwilling to work over the weekend. She went to my boss and he did it for her instead. I must find other ways to respond in future.

YOUR REFLECTIONS

STEP 1: RECONSTRUCT THE MAP

- Discover which side of the paradox you lean more toward.
- Do a reality check on what is working (or not) in your circumstances.
- Answer in detail. If you are unsure, review the example.

A. Which is more important to you most often, tasks or people?

B. Under what circumstances does your preference change? Why?

C. On a scale of 1 to 10 (*1 being worst and 10 being best*), how effective is your approach? What are your thoughts on your score?

D. What needs to happen to increase the score?

SERENE'S REFLECTIONS

STEP 2: REFRESH THE LENS

A. What is the reality for you right now?

My family life is going well. My career not so much. I have been in this role for five years, with positive performance reviews each year. But something is preventing my chances of promotion. I am not ready to leave this job as the flexibility complements my family life.

If I do not respond to the feedback from the 360 assessment, I believe I will be stuck here.

B. How do you want this reality to change in the next 6 months?

I want to at least get started on the path to a promotion or an expansion in my job scope. I am tired of doing the same thing.

It's time to change, grow and develop. Even if the organization is not ready to promote me, I want to prepare myself and develop other useful skills in the meantime.

C. What are the non-negotiables in what you want to achieve or become?

- Career growth and expansion in job scope. Either I take over another portfolio or become a people-leader.
- My family time and autonomy over the use of my time
- Efficiency in delivering on tasks and holding people accountable for quality and timely work.

D. In relation to your answer to Question C, what is the missing ingredient in your current reality?

If I want to be a people-leader, I need to build better relationships. In fact, it is one of the corporate values and corporate dimensions I was rated on. Collaboration and teamwork mean a lot in our environment.

My manager's support is another ingredient I need. I need him to champion and support me in my aspirations. I know he is not entirely pleased with me now. I should consider changing that.

If I work on building relationships on all fronts, it will probably improve my chances in securing my next career move within the organization.

YOUR REFLECTIONS

STEP 2: REFRESH THE LENS

- Determine the real impact of past behavior.
- Decide what is needed now.
- Clearly describe your ideal state.

A. What is the reality for you right now?

B. How do you want this reality to change in the next 6 months?

C. What are the non-negotiables in what you want to achieve or become?

D. In relation to your answer to Question C, what is the missing ingredient in your current reality?

SERENE'S REFLECTIONS

STEP 3: RENEW THE IDENTITY

A. Describe your current state using a metaphor.

I see myself as a small plant growing in the cracks of a pavement. My deep roots represent my commitment to my family. My roots are extensive, representing the experience and credibility gained in my career.

B. Describe your ideal self using a new metaphor. Draw it here.

My new metaphor is a dandelion which can cast its seeds far and wide, representing my aspiration to grow in influence.

C. Explore shifts in mindset required for you to move from the old to the new metaphor.

Old metaphor

- I have limited influence as I operate from a remote location.
- I do not have face-time with the stakeholders.
- Building relationships virtually is not as easy as in person.
- I am fast and quick.
- I am a taskmaster.

New metaphor

- I can find ways to increase my influence regardless of where I am.
- I can build relationships with stakeholders by communicating appropriately.
- I can be creative in the manner I connect virtually.
- I can be fast and responsive and also diplomatic.
- I am gentle and assertive, empathetic and effective.

YOUR REFLECTIONS

STEP 3: RENEW THE IDENTITY

- Create a strong mental image of the identity you want to embrace.
- Give the new identity life by exploring possible shifts in mindset.
- Design initial actions.

A. Describe your current state using a metaphor.

B. Describe your ideal self using a new metaphor. Draw it here.

C. Explore shifts in mindset required for you to move from the old to the new metaphor.

Old metaphor

New metaphor

SERENE'S REFLECTIONS

STEP 4: REBUILD THE CAPABILITIES

A. As part of your new identity, what actions can you start taking? Why?

I can be creative in how I handle virtual calls. Perhaps I can begin with small talk, or ask about their family or children. So many conversation starters! I can also switch on my video camera and dress up for the call. It might show I care about the people with whom I connect.

When the team sends email invites for weekend or middle-of-the-night calls, I can reply with a cordial email reminding them of my different time zone instead of declining the invitation without offering reasons. If they cannot accommodate my timing, I will read the minutes and clarify any doubts. If they ask for an extension of deadlines I will give reasons if it cannot be done.

I will give myself 12 to 24 hours to respond to emails instead of responding immediately. I want to show my manager that I value his feedback about responding instead of reacting too quickly.

B. What might be hard to do? How can you overcome the difficulty?

Given my reputation and image, becoming friendly suddenly will be the biggest hurdle. I should practice my conversation starters aloud before a mirror or say them to my husband, to see if they sound natural. Preparation is important.

Not responding to emails immediately will be difficult. Usually when my phone pings, I respond. I will turn off notifications and only check my emails at 3 pm and 7 pm each day. I will also draft my replies but send them only the next day.

C. How will you know your actions are effective?

I will observe the reactions of my teammates during our meetings. I will give myself five to six sessions before I restrategize.

If I start feeling less uncomfortable, and they share more about their personal lives, I will know I am on the right track.

I will inform my manager that I am working on improving the tone of my emails and ask for his feedback at our weekly one-on-one meetings.

YOUR REFLECTIONS

STEP 4: REBUILD THE CAPABILITIES

- Design actions that will help you actualize the new metaphor.
- Practice the actions in small steps so you can reach your goal progressively.

A. As part of your new identity, what actions can you start taking? Why?

B. What might be hard to do? How can you overcome the difficulty?

C. How will you know your actions are effective?

INDIVIDUALS vs TEAMS

TIM

PROFILE

- A veteran team leader in a foreign IT firm.
- Previously experienced a lot of success in a large local IT firm with a similar set-up.
- Managed an underperforming member in the team without much success.
- Neglected some collaboration requests from another team.
- Failed to give adequate attention to the rest of his team.

CHALLENGE

Received a long, negative peer review, and his leadership effectiveness came into question.

GOALS

To meet the expectations of his superiors and to manage his relationships with his team and his peers.

See how Tim navigated the paradox using the Re4 Coaching Model.

TIM'S REFLECTIONS

STEP 1: RECONSTRUCT THE MAP

A. How do individuals and teams interact within your context?

Each individual on the team performs similar roles but for different accounts. All have different strengths and ways of managing work. They offer help, advice or coaching when needed. My role is to help my team succeed. When we meet our targets, it is due to the contribution of each one. Without individuals, there is no team.

B. How do these relationships affect the performance of individuals and the team?

The team is cohesive. They coach, support and cover for each other willingly even if it may mean taking on more work for a period.

Though there is healthy competition, they learn best practices from one another so the team can succeed. But there are stragglers, such as Ryan. I have been trying to coach him but it's taken up so much of my attention, I am neglecting my team.

C. On a scale of 1 to 10 (*1 being worst and 10 being best*), how effective is your approach? What are your thoughts on your score?

I would say I am at 3. The team's performance has slowed and Ryan has not improved despite coaching and assistance. With Ryan not pulling his weight, there is definitely resentment among the team.

I feel stretched. I want to help Ryan as best as I can, but I also feel responsible to my team. A few times, I was not there when they needed me for decisions. Additionally, I received a negative review from my peer due to this — I had brushed her off as I was busy trying to coach Ryan. I missed an important deadline which impacted her team negatively. She saw me as uncooperative and lodged a complaint. My approach has not benefited the team nor me, and certainly not Ryan.

D. What needs to happen to increase the score?

- Tilt the balance towards the bigger picture and share my time and attention across areas that matter.
- Regain the faith of my leaders!
- Reconsider if Ryan is suited for the job. Ultimately, this might not help in his career development. I should speak with him about this.

YOUR REFLECTIONS

STEP 1: RECONSTRUCT THE MAP

- Discover which side of the paradox you lean more toward.
- Do a reality check on what is working (or not) in your circumstances.
- Answer in detail. If you are unsure, review the example.

A. How do individuals and teams interact within your context?

B. How do these relationships affect the performance of individuals and the team?

C. On a scale of 1 to 10 (*1 being worst and 10 being best*), how effective is your approach? What are your thoughts on your score?

D. What needs to happen to increase the score?

TIM'S REFLECTIONS

STEP 2: REFRESH THE LENS

A. What is the reality for you right now?

I am not gaining any traction with my superior, my peers, my team or with Ryan. What is even more disturbing is, I am also getting nowhere with myself. This has to stop if I mean to save my career.

B. How do you want this reality to change in the next 6 months?

I want all individuals to function at their best so our team can succeed. This also means that I play my part to develop and support them well. Looking at the bigger picture, I want to work towards having my team collaborate with other teams seamlessly. I must take time to focus on bridging and facilitating this.

As a people-leader, I must develop and support everyone according to their career path. I should have a clearer sight of each person's goals instead of the fuzzy ideas I have right now.

I want to also show my superiors that I am discerning and able to make the right judgment calls for my team and the organization.

C. What are the non-negotiables in what you want to achieve or become?

- Regain the trust of my superior.
- Repair the relationship with my colleague and help her see that her team can count on my team. Rebuilding that communication channel is critical.
- Ensure the growth and success of my team. I will devote more time to developing the individuals on my team and help them progress in their careers instead of focusing only on Ryan.

D. In relation to your answer to Question C, what is the missing ingredient in your current reality?

The missing ingredient is the ability to acknowledge that I might not be the one who can develop Ryan, or that Ryan might not be the right person for this role. Part of me refused to give up and call it quits, and was attacking the issue with brute force. I need to start thinking about this differently.

YOUR REFLECTIONS

STEP 2: REFRESH THE LENS

- Determine the real impact of past behavior.
- Decide what is needed now.
- Clearly describe your ideal state.

A. What is the reality for you right now?

B. How do you want this reality to change in the next 6 months?

C. What are the non-negotiables in what you want to achieve or become?

D. In relation to your answer to Question C, what is the missing ingredient in your current reality?

TIM'S REFLECTIONS

STEP 3: RENEW THE IDENTITY

A. Describe your current state using a metaphor.

I have been too deeply entrenched in one particular situation, too focused on getting one individual to perform at his level best.
I missed other important parts.
I used to think I am like a person leading a team of people up a flight of stairs, believing that we are scaling greater heights.

B. Describe your ideal self using a new metaphor. Draw it here.

My new metaphor is the Penrose stairs — a reminder that while I think I am climbing up, I might be going in circles or heading downwards instead.
I need to step out of the illusion and step into reality, with a clarity of perspective.

C. Explore shifts in mindset required for you to move from the old to the new metaphor.

Old metaphor

- I want to personally coach every individual to help each one to perform at his best.
- If I put in more time to work with individuals, they will improve.
- My responsibility is to ensure my team performs well.

New metaphor

- I can involve strong team members to coach others, so every individual can perform at his best.
- Investing time and effort in an individual may not bring about a proportional improvement. I must know when to stop.
- My responsibility is to ensure my team (including me) performs and works well with other teams.

YOUR REFLECTIONS

STEP 3: RENEW THE IDENTITY

- Create a strong mental image of the identity you want to embrace.
- Give the new identity life by exploring possible shifts in mindset.
- Design initial actions.

A. Describe your current state using a metaphor.

B. Describe your ideal self using a new metaphor. Draw it here.

C. Explore shifts in mindset required for you to move from the old to the new metaphor.

Old metaphor

New metaphor

TIM'S REFLECTIONS

STEP 4: REBUILD THE CAPABILITIES

A. As part of your new identity, what actions can you start taking? Why?

I will invest time to repair the relationship with my colleague. I accept her feedback and take responsibility for my lapse. This is crucial to getting our teams to cooperate well again. With my team, I will have regular one-on-ones and focus on developing them.

I will bring Ryan's issue to my superiors' attention and propose an intervention plan where a high potential will coach Ryan with me for 6 months. After that, I will decide if we should keep him.

I want to share my learning with my superiors so I can regain their trust. It is best to be authentic and take responsibility for my lapses.

B. What might be hard to do? How can you overcome the difficulty?

Repairing the relationship with my colleague is the most difficult. Her feedback took me completely by surprise as she had not mentioned anything to me directly before sending that damaging review to my superiors. I am going to be the 'better' person here, and acknowledge that there have been lapses on my part. I want an open relationship between us. I need to plan and propose a way of working which we can discuss and agree on.

For Ryan, the thought of letting him go feels cruel. I want to come up with an intervention process, keeping in mind that I am also responsible for the other individuals on the team. It is not justifiable to sacrifice those individuals (and the team) for him. Once I get my superiors' support, I will have an honest discussion with Ryan.

C. How will you know your actions are effective?

Getting endorsement from my superiors is the first indicator. If they agree with my intervention plan for Ryan and my intention to repair the relationship with my colleague, I will be assured I'm on the right track. I will also gauge my progress from the response of my colleague. Rebuilding cooperation will take time, so I will be prompt in follow-up.

As for Ryan, I want to engage both him and the high potential I have identified. We will continue our regular one-on-ones and I will gauge if the intervention plan is effective.

YOUR REFLECTIONS

STEP 4: REBUILD THE CAPABILITIES

- Design actions that will help you actualize the new metaphor.
- Practice the actions in small steps so you can reach your goal progressively.

A. As part of your new identity, what actions can you start taking? Why?

B. What might be hard to do? How can you overcome the difficulty?

C. How will you know your actions are effective?

SELF vs SYSTEM

AMY

PROFILE

- A devoted in-house recruiter.
- Carried a strong sense of duty and mission towards her role.
- Worked across a few time zones to be responsive to the team.
- Worked very long hours; signs of being an absent spouse and parent.

CHALLENGE

Overwhelmed with guilt both at work and at home; experienced panic attacks.

GOALS

To stop being overwhelmed by guilt and perform well as a whole person.

See how Amy navigated the paradox using the Re4 Coaching Model.

AMY'S REFLECTIONS

STEP 1: RECONSTRUCT THE MAP

A. What are the different versions of 'you' in your life?

At work, I'm a dynamic, reliable, trusted partner to a few business units. I ensure the best talents are sourced so business can thrive. I'm on a mission to give the job to the best person. When I send the letter of offer, I often think, "This letter will change someone's life."

In my personal life, I'm an overworked and guilt-ridden wife and mother. My social life is non-existent. I often feel inadequate, with nothing to give. My children's crying and the never-ending housework drive me crazy. I try my best at home, but I often feel useless, over-stretched and exhausted. I wish my house was self-cleaning and my children would grow up sooner! The thought of going home to the chaos depresses me. I am ashamed to admit it.

B. How does the 'system' define 'you'?

At work, I'm respected. People count on me. I'm known for my dedication and strong sense of mission. At home, my husband is frustrated with me. My children are probably too young to understand, but I fear their childhood memories of me will be that I am always on a laptop or phone, unavailable to them.

The difference between my home and work contexts is alarming. Honestly, I don't know who I am. It definitely feels like my job defines me. This does not make sense as my family is more important to me.

C. On a scale of 1 to 10 (*1 being worst and 10 being best*), how effective is your approach in handling the demands of the 'system' in which you work? What are your thoughts on your score?

This is so difficult. I would score myself a 2. My professional identity and personal self are too different. My husband said once too many times that I am married to my job. I need to remember that I am a whole person. I want a holistic life. My life will be meaningless if I do not have a strong relationship with my family.

D. What needs to happen to increase the score?

I need to focus on myself and not be ruled by a sense of duty to my job and my team. I can be committed to my job, but also to my family and my children.

YOUR REFLECTIONS

STEP 1: RECONSTRUCT THE MAP

- Discover which side of the paradox you lean more toward.
- Do a reality check on what is working (or not) in your circumstances.
- Answer in detail. If you are unsure, review the example.

A. What are the different versions of 'you' in your life?

B. How does the 'system' define 'you'?

C. On a scale of 1 to 10 (*1 being worst and 10 being best*), how effective is your approach in handling the demands of the 'system' in which you work? What are your thoughts on your score?

D. What needs to happen to increase the score?

AMY'S REFLECTIONS

STEP 2: REFRESH THE LENS

A. What is the reality for you right now?

At work, I am doing my best to make a difference in the lives of others. This is largely absent in my personal life as I feel I have nothing to give. Perhaps that is why I avoid playing the role of a mother and a wife — because I feel like I am failing miserably at it. It is not a good feeling to have.

I feel out of sync, toggling between the elation of being successful at work and feeling like a good-for-nothing at home. I frequently feel tired and burdened. I feel rushed at work and at home. My mood is at a constant low.

B. How do you want this reality to change in the next 6 months?

I want to stop feeling overwhelmed. I want to have calm and satisfaction that is constant, and a healthy dose of humility to know my human limits. I want to be okay with the days when I am less than perfect, to know I have someone to rely on or to cover for me when I am unable to manage. I want greater consistency in moods and greater balance in my life.

C. What are the non-negotiables in what you want to achieve or become?

My relationship with my children is non-negotiable. My life will be full of regrets if we do not have a deep relationship. I want to be a part of their happy memories and to do that, I need my husband's support to make this happen.

I still want to succeed in my career and be the one who changes someone's life. But I can do this without sacrificing my personal life.

D. In relation to your answer to Question C, what is the missing ingredient in your current reality?

What is missing was the discernment that my desire to make a difference to others in my professional life took away my ability to do so in my personal life. I was also not courageous enough to have the conversations needed to resolve the frustrations in my personal life.

YOUR REFLECTIONS

STEP 2: REFRESH THE LENS

- Determine the real impact of past behavior.
- Decide what is needed now.
- Clearly describe your ideal state.

A. What is the reality for you right now?

B. How do you want this reality to change in the next 6 months?

C. What are the non-negotiables in what you want to achieve or become?

D. In relation to your answer to Question C, what is the missing ingredient in your current reality?

AMY'S REFLECTIONS

STEP 3: RENEW THE IDENTITY

A. Describe your current state using a metaphor.

My metaphor for my current state is the sun. It touches everything everywhere. It is limitless. While it is a beautiful metaphor, I think that is not a sustainable state for me.

B. Describe your ideal self using a new metaphor. Draw it here.

My new metaphor is a candle casting light in a room. I need to remember that I am limited in my effect and resources. My job is to light what is in the room and that includes my family. To cast light for others, I need to have something left to give.

C. Explore shifts in mindset required for you to move from the old to the new metaphor.

Old metaphor

- I will work very long, very hard, as there are so many lives waiting for me to transform and to make a difference for.
- I make a difference to people only through my work.

New metaphor

- I can do my best and make a difference to someone if I am feeling my best. So I need to take care of myself in all aspects.
- I am living a holistic life so I can make a difference to all the lives I touch and that includes myself, my family and friends.

YOUR REFLECTIONS

STEP 3: RENEW THE IDENTITY

- Create a strong mental image of the identity you want to embrace.
- Give the new identity life by exploring possible shifts in mindset.
- Design initial actions.

A. Describe your current state using a metaphor.

B. Describe your ideal self using a new metaphor. Draw it here.

C. Explore shifts in mindset required for you to move from the old to the new metaphor.

Old metaphor

New metaphor

AMY'S REFLECTIONS

STEP 4: REBUILD THE CAPABILITIES

A. As part of your new identity, what actions can you start taking? Why?

I want to refocus on leading a holistic life, and make a clear distinction between my professional and personal life. I want to discuss with my spouse how I can make a difference at home and work out an arrangement that suits us.

At work, I need to start setting boundaries. I will focus on people I can reach, be thankful for those I can make a difference for. I will assign a specific time for work and keep within it. I will not allow myself to burn out entirely for work.

B. What might be hard to do? How can you overcome the difficulty?

The compulsion to be always available for my colleagues and not be seen as a bottleneck is most difficult. I have a personal brand of being reliable and responsive, so this is going to take effort to rework.

As I set boundaries, I will weigh consequences: if I am responsive to only one aspect of my life, what will the impact be to another aspect?

I also want to mindfully shift into the metaphor of being a candle and to recognize that I do not have unlimited energy to give. I need to take care of myself so I can shine for a long, long time.

C. How will you know your actions are effective?

The indicators that will tell me my actions are effective will be:
- my daily energy level
- my ability to focus on tasks
- my mood

I will start implementing the changes and monitor my progress week-on-week.

YOUR REFLECTIONS

STEP 4: REBUILD THE CAPABILITIES

- Design actions that will help you actualize the new metaphor.
- Practice the actions in small steps so you can reach your goal progressively.

A. As part of your new identity, what actions can you start taking? Why?

B. What might be hard to do? How can you overcome the difficulty?

C. How will you know your actions are effective?

LEADING vs FOLLOWING

CHRISTOPHER

PROFILE

- A director in a large internet software company.
- Led a team of subject-matter experts.
- Identified his strengths as being articulate and strategic, and supportive towards his team.
- Tried to be both an individual contributor and a leader at the same time, without much success.

CHALLENGE

Motivation was waning; struggled to see his value as a leader because he was not as technically skilled as his team members.

GOALS

To stay motivated in his role, find creative ways to lead and contribute, and raise his leadership influence.

See how Christopher navigated the paradox using the Re4 Coaching Model.

CHRISTOPHER'S REFLECTIONS

STEP 1: RECONSTRUCT THE MAP

A. What irreplaceable value does your team of experts bring to the organization?

Our domain is highly volatile and my team of experts each bring a different skill, giving us a competitive advantage. They are a rare breed — technically competent with a drive to push boundaries and reinvent the work we do. This is invaluable and irreplaceable.

B. What irreplaceable value do you bring to your team and organization?

I bring industry knowledge and strategic thinking. I provide the big picture and direction. I have been in this field long enough to predict trends and identify where to invest resources to gain a competitive advantage. My team counts on me to support them. No conversation is too difficult for me. If they need me to negotiate, I will. If they need clear direction, I will find it. I am excellent at managing stakeholders — something my team does not enjoy — so they value this quality.

My manager and I are well-aligned. He knows I am a person of integrity and he entrusts the team to me, knowing I will make the best decision for the organization and my team. My team also knows I will fairly acknowledge their achievements to my manager.

C. On a scale of 1 to 10 (*1 being worst and 10 being best*), how effective is your approach? What are your thoughts on your score?

My overall effectiveness is 6 out of 10. The earlier questions made me realize I still bring a lot of irreplaceable value to the team and organization. I also see how my team and I complement each other. Things are better than I had thought. Despite how I was feeling, my team is functioning very well.

D. What needs to happen to increase the score?

I should identify other ways that only I can contribute. Career development is important to my team. I can set the stage for them to shine and prepare them for the next level in their career. I will follow their lead where they have expertise and trust their judgment (like my manager trusts me). I also need to acknowledge myself more as being critical of myself isn't helpful my team or to me.

YOUR REFLECTIONS

STEP 1: RECONSTRUCT THE MAP

- Discover which side of the paradox you lean more toward.
- Do a reality check on what is working (or not) in your circumstances.
- Answer in detail. If you are unsure, review the example.

A. What irreplaceable value does your team of experts bring to the organization?

B. What irreplaceable value do you bring to your team and organization?

C. On a scale of 1 to 10 (*1 being worst and 10 being best*), how effective is your approach? What are your thoughts on your score?

D. What needs to happen to increase the score?

CHRISTOPHER'S REFLECTIONS

STEP 2: REFRESH THE LENS

A. What is the reality for you right now?

I am trying to be the leader and individual contributor at once. This is unrealistic, given the time it takes to develop subject-matter expertise at that depth in just one domain. Instead of focusing on the value I can bring, I'm focusing on what I lack. This affects how I interact with the team. I've become depressed; my motivation is waning. But in reality, things aren't as bad as I'd thought they were. I have strong support from my manager and some team members. Perhaps a few are more judgmental, but I'll not go far if what I want is their approval.

B. How do you want this reality to change in the next 6 months?

I want to focus on what I do best, providing strategic direction and support so my team can thrive. I want to change the way I feel when I am with the team. I want to be okay with 'not being the smartest person' in the room, to feel secure and lead them in my own way.

I want to be flexible and humble — sometimes leading, sometimes letting my team take the lead. While I provide strategic direction, they provide expert knowledge. I do not need to always have the last say or to always know the answer. There will always be something I don't know, and I want to be okay with that. This is also an opportunity for my team to take charge and to shine.

C. What are the non-negotiables in what you want to achieve or become?

The success of my team and my continuous learning are non-negotiables. I shouldn't be the hindrance to the success of my team, even if I'm technically less knowledgeable. Even though the playing field is not level (I am learning something my younger colleagues had learned in school), I am not going to let it hinder my growth.

D. In relation to your answer to Question C, what is the missing ingredient in your current reality?

Being able to do everything on my own is unnecessary and not sustainable. I am not supposed to be a one-man army. I was unwilling to be vulnerable. So moving forward, I will allow myself to be vulnerable, to be human.

YOUR REFLECTIONS

STEP 2: REFRESH THE LENS

- Determine the real impact of past behavior.
- Decide what is needed now.
- Clearly describe your ideal state.

A. What is the reality for you right now?

B. How do you want this reality to change in the next 6 months?

C. What are the non-negotiables in what you want to achieve or become?

D. In relation to your answer to Question C, what is the missing ingredient in your current reality?

CHRISTOPHER'S REFLECTIONS

STEP 3: RENEW THE IDENTITY

A. Describe your current state using a metaphor.

I used to expect myself to be a Swiss army knife. I need all the tools, but I do not have them all. In reality, it will take too much time to acquire all the know-how to become a Swiss army knife.

B. Describe your ideal self using a new metaphor. Draw it here.

My new metaphor is a toolbox. I'm a tool in this toolbox, together with the other tools (the members of my team). Sometimes I might be a hammer and sometimes a saw. It depends on the context. I can discern which tool is best suited for each situation. As a team, we can create many things together.

C. Explore shifts in mindset required for you to move from the old to the new metaphor.

Old metaphor

- I alone have to accomplish everything.
- I am not worthy of leading this team as I am technically less knowledgeable.
- If I cannot do something, I cannot expect my team to do it.

New metaphor

- I lead my team to accomplish everything together.
- I bring wisdom and strategy to this team, something that makes me the right person to lead the team.
- My team and I complement each other. I expect them to take the lead in the areas of their expertise and I support them to make things happen.

YOUR REFLECTIONS

STEP 3: RENEW THE IDENTITY

- Create a strong mental image of the identity you want to embrace.
- Give the new identity life by exploring possible shifts in mindset.
- Design initial actions.

A. Describe your current state using a metaphor.

B. Describe your ideal self using a new metaphor. Draw it here.

C. Explore shifts in mindset required for you to move from the old to the new metaphor.

Old metaphor

New metaphor

CHRISTOPHER'S REFLECTIONS

STEP 4: REBUILD THE CAPABILITIES

A. As part of your new identity, what actions can you start taking? Why?

I can start by clearly defining what success looks like to me. I want to align this with my team's expectations of me. This will also mean I need to set the context clearly with them, so they know my limitations, how I am committed to learning from them, to following their lead, and my thankfulness that they allow me to be their leader.

I also want to clearly articulate the value I bring to the team, the strategic focus, and how I want to support them in their career development and raise our team performance to the next level. When I face areas I am unsure about, I want to ask my team for their expert advice.

I want to introduce a daily gratitude exercise that gets me in the right mode. At the end of the day, I want to review my day and affirm myself for the right things I have done.

B. What might be hard to do? How can you overcome the difficulty?

Hearing the expectations of my team might be difficult for me at the start. Showing my vulnerability might also be challenging.

I want to engage some of the team members who are more supportive of me now, and listen to their feedback. I will want to do some role-plays in our coaching sessions so you can highlight some of my blind spots.

C. How will you know your actions are effective?

If the selected team members approve (endorse) my thinking, I know I am likely on the right track. Thereafter, I will know if the team is receptive towards me, if they come to me for advice and if they value my input.

I will also know my actions are effective if I end the day with more 'positives' than 'negatives' and with an increased feeling that I have been able to lead and add value to my team.

YOUR REFLECTIONS

STEP 4: REBUILD THE CAPABILITIES

- Design actions that will help you actualize the new metaphor.
- Practice the actions in small steps so you can reach your goal progressively.

A. As part of your new identity, what actions can you start taking? Why?

B. What might be hard to do? How can you overcome the difficulty?

C. How will you know your actions are effective?

BOTTOM-UP vs TOP-DOWN

ADELINE

PROFILE

- An agile coach in a large corporation with a long legacy and a conservative culture.
- Aimed to drive change and bring agile practices into 20 percent of the organization in a year.
- Enjoyed working with teams where the action was.
- Worked mostly alone to introduce agile practices.

CHALLENGE

Efforts met with poor results. Faced resistance from middle managers and did not enjoy full support from senior management due to a lack of tangible results.

GOALS

To increase the impact of the transformation and speed up the pace of change with greater economy of effort.

See how Adeline navigated the paradox using the Re4 Coaching Model.

ADELINE'S REFLECTIONS

STEP 1: RECONSTRUCT THE MAP

A. How are you driving change now using the bottom-up approach?

I am trying to drive change by working with people on the ground, showing them how things can be done differently. I set structures in place and help them internalize habits till they eventually become advocates and change agents.

B. How are you driving change now using the top-down approach?

I am working on this indirectly. The senior management brought me in because they had a vision that things could be different and wanted me to drive change in the organization. Though supportive in principle, they need convincing.

My strategy is to create success stories from the teams to show how the organization can be transformed by taking bolder steps. I update management regularly on progress and pace of adoption, keeping in mind the goal to increase the percentage of projects completed in the agile approach from 5 to 20 percent by next year.

We identify the business units or project teams to include in the pilot. That has gone moderately well. Some middle managers are supportive, though not all.

C. On a scale of 1 to 10 (*1 being worst and 10 being best*), how effective is your approach? What are your thoughts on your score?

I rate my effectiveness at 5. My strategy to create success stories at the team level requires me to put in more hours. The more teams I work with, the more thinly I spread myself. Senior and middle management sometimes express expectations that are counterproductive and set back my efforts. I am always trying to catch up and fight fires. My efforts are not translating into results. I've seen some traction but not enough to reach the 20 percent target.

D. What needs to happen to increase the score?

I need to align the bottom-up and top-down approach. We can first try to reduce any top-down emphasis that are counterproductive to what the teams are experimenting with, so that the rate of change can be improved with greater collaboration.

YOUR REFLECTIONS

STEP 1: RECONSTRUCT THE MAP

- Discover which side of the paradox you lean more toward.
- Do a reality check on what is working (or not) in your circumstances.
- Answer in detail. If you are unsure, review the example.

A. How are you driving change now using the bottom-up approach?

B. How are you driving change now using the top-down approach?

C. On a scale of 1 to 10 (*1 being worst and 10 being best*), how effective is your approach? What are your thoughts on your score?

D. What needs to happen to increase the score?

ADELINE'S REFLECTIONS

STEP 2: REFRESH THE LENS

A. What is the reality for you right now?

I am spreading myself too thin, and the task seems too difficult. While I'd like to increase the target from 20 percent, right now even that seems unattainable. All I have built seems to be going to waste. I flip-flop between giving up and trudging on just because I am passionate about agility. I feel I'm taking on this task alone. I have been telling the senior management that I need more support from the middle managers and more resources (like more coaches), but I am not getting any until I can show results. It is a vicious cycle.

B. How do you want this reality to change in the next 6 months?

I want to see greater collaboration between bottom-up and top-down forces, to have more resources and develop a pool of advocates with whom to discuss ideas and challenges. I want to see transformation take place in a strategic, united manner. Teams should be independent and supported by their superiors. I want to begin a cycle of positive change and showcase it. I should take on the most challenging teams and those that can generate the best results and showcase them to gain more support from the senior management.

C. What are the non-negotiables in what you want to achieve or become?

To be an effective agile coach and make a positive change in the organization. Reaching the 20 percent is a non-negotiable, minimum target. I also want to leave a legacy for the organization as I believe in its mission. My contributions here should persist even after I have left.

D. In relation to your answer to Question C, what is the missing ingredient in your current reality?

The missing ingredient is the top-down support at the team level (middle managers). Support from the top senior management will depend on whether teams can generate success stories. I can, however, create an environment so the teams receive more top-down support from the middle managers, and work bottom-up as well, so that at least at the team level, there is greater convergence between the top-down and bottom-up approach.

YOUR REFLECTIONS

STEP 2: REFRESH THE LENS

- Determine the real impact of past behavior.
- Decide what is needed now.
- Clearly describe your ideal state.

A. What is the reality for you right now?

B. How do you want this reality to change in the next 6 months?

C. What are the non-negotiables in what you want to achieve or become?

D. In relation to your answer to Question C, what is the missing ingredient in your current reality?

ADELINE'S REFLECTIONS

STEP 3: RENEW THE IDENTITY

A. Describe your current state using a metaphor.

I see myself as a spider web, stretched very thin. As I try to advocate change with more teams, I cover a greater area, but I am dangerously close to tearing apart.

B. Describe your ideal self using a new metaphor. Draw it here.

My new metaphor is a network repeater — a device that replicates and relays signals along a network. I am no longer working alone but in a network, with an informal team of influencers.

C. Explore shifts in mindset required for you to move from the old to the new metaphor.

Old metaphor

- I am the only one who can initiate the transformation.
- I can only get the strong top-down support when I have enough success stories at the team level.
- I need to work with every team personally.

New metaphor

- I can create a pool of advocates and initiate the change together.
- I can have different levels of support: at team level, the top-down support comes from middle managers; at the senior management level, the bottom-up support/ advocacy comes from middle managers.
- With a pool of advocates, I can divide and conquer, leaving time for me to work with high-stakes teams that require more attention.

YOUR REFLECTIONS

STEP 3: RENEW THE IDENTITY

- Create a strong mental image of the identity you want to embrace.
- Give the new identity life by exploring possible shifts in mindset.
- Design initial actions.

A. Describe your current state using a metaphor.

B. Describe your ideal self using a new metaphor. Draw it here.

C. Explore shifts in mindset required for you to move from the old to the new metaphor.

Old metaphor

New metaphor

ADELINE'S REFLECTIONS

STEP 4: REBUILD THE CAPABILITIES

A. As part of your new identity, what actions can you start taking? Why?

I can identify innovative department heads (middle managers) who are enthusiastic about enterprise transformations. Off the top of my head, I can identify the Head of Supply Chain and Head of Customer Relations, who have always been interested in my work. The teams they oversee are currently undergoing the transformation with some resistance, so support from these Heads will be helpful. I will set up some meetings with them and together, we will envision how things can be different at the department level and establish more supporting structures to enable the transformation. I will also speak about the opportunity for them to advocate for transformation to the senior management. In this way, the success stories will not come from me alone.

Some scrum masters have been doing well. I will look into training them to be agile coaches. I will begin these conversations next week. I will work smarter instead of working harder.

B. What might be hard to do? How can you overcome the difficulty?

Given my impatience and eagerness to speed up the transformation, I know I will feel the urge to do more personally. I will remind myself that my goal is to create other 'network repeaters', a group of advocates, and not do the work myself.

I want to focus on sustainability so I can last longer in the arena. For the transformation to be successful and to reach the target of 20 percent, I need both a bottom-up and top-down approach.

C. How will you know your actions are effective?

I will know the actions are effective when the pool of advocates increases. For now, I am on my own. In two weeks, I want to form a task force, and together, come up with a strategy that will transform one department at a time, facilitating change from both top-down and bottom-up. Over time, the task force will grow in size and I will then have more advocates driving change from their respective roles and have enough success stories to share and fully convince the senior management.

YOUR REFLECTIONS

STEP 4: REBUILD THE CAPABILITIES

- Design actions that will help you actualize the new metaphor.
- Practice the actions in small steps so you can reach your goal progressively.

A. As part of your new identity, what actions can you start taking? Why?

B. What might be hard to do? How can you overcome the difficulty?

C. How will you know your actions are effective?

EXECUTING vs INSPIRING

PRAKASH

PROFILE

- A technical leader and advisor to top management.
- Respected and well-liked, pleasant and easy-going.
- Worked with a group of technical experts as a peer and advisor.
- Wished to improve customer satisfaction by changing the way technical experts operated — by using data from customer cases and eliminating faults in future products.

CHALLENGE

In a deadlock with the team of technical experts as they did not see the purpose of revolutionizing the way they had been working.

GOALS

To increase his ability to influence and inspire the team to make a difficult but strategic change.

See how Prakash navigated the paradox using the Re4 Coaching Model.

PRAKASH'S REFLECTIONS

STEP 1: RECONSTRUCT THE MAP

A. What is the real reason you want this change in the team?

I believe the future of the organization lies in this change I am trying to drive. Looking at current market trends, we need to change how we work. It will bring a competitive advantage to the company as well as benefits for individual employees.

This organization has inspired me with its mission and vision for the past 15 years that I have worked here. I have grown so much here. I want this team to also learn and grow as I have.

B. What do you think is the team's understanding of the change required?

The team probably sees the steps I am asking them to do as additional work. They complained that the data we have amassed from the customer cases is so massive, just to filter and organize them will take much time. The effort they have to put in to sieve through the data, coordinate with the relevant departments and to propose changes in future products is more real to them than any nebulous 'improvement' in their future. I could see from their faces that they do not welcome the extra work, so I doubt they understood the rationale for it.

C. On a scale of 1 to 10 (*1 being worst and 10 being best*), how effective is your approach? What are your thoughts on your score?

I rate my effectiveness as 4 out of 10. There is more resistance than buy-in. The team questions the need for change as the process we now have seems good enough. They don't see how reducing the percentage of cases escalated (and better customer satisfaction) can benefit them. To help them, I added more steps so the process will be more effective. I created checklists and instruction sheets so they will not miss anything.

D. What needs to happen to increase the score?

I need to help the team understand the goal and the value behind this work. To get their buy-in and involve them in creating a vision worth pursuing and actualizing, I need to begin a dialogue and share this dream I have, and help them see how things can be different.

YOUR REFLECTIONS

STEP 1: RECONSTRUCT THE MAP

- Discover which side of the paradox you lean more toward.
- Do a reality check on what is working (or not) in your circumstances.
- Answer in detail. If you are unsure, review the example.

A. What is the real reason you want this change in the team?

B. What do you think is the team's understanding of the change required?

C. On a scale of 1 to 10 (*1 being worst and 10 being best*), how effective is your approach? What are your thoughts on your score?

D. What needs to happen to increase the score?

PRAKASH'S REFLECTIONS

STEP 2: REFRESH THE LENS

A. What is the reality for you right now?

I feel fully responsible for this vision and I feel like I am dealing with too many unexpected behaviors that derail me. Every time that happens, I add on more processes to mitigate those issues, but I wonder if this is effective.

I see fatigue in the team as they mechanically follow the processes I set. It seems like a paper exercise to them. At the same time, I cannot hold them accountable as they do not report to me.

B. How do you want this reality to change in the next 6 months?

I want to see everyone take ownership to refine the process, meet the challenges and improve the way we design our products so that we can see higher customer satisfaction and fewer escalations of problems.

I believe the team has good ideas and I want to draw them out. I believe by putting our heads together, we can see positive changes, which will not only make their work less hectic but also increase the value and impact.

C. What are the non-negotiables in what you want to achieve or become?

Teamwork is a non-negotiable. I can only accomplish so much alone. My role as a strategic advisor is to propose how we can use data to improve product design, but the process should be owned by the team.

D. In relation to your answer to Question C, what is the missing ingredient in your current reality?

The buy-in and full participation from the team is missing now.

YOUR REFLECTIONS

STEP 2: REFRESH THE LENS

- Determine the real impact of past behavior.
- Decide what is needed now.
- Clearly describe your ideal state.

A. What is the reality for you right now?

B. How do you want this reality to change in the next 6 months?

C. What are the non-negotiables in what you want to achieve or become?

D. In relation to your answer to Question C, what is the missing ingredient in your current reality?

PRAKASH'S REFLECTIONS

STEP 3: RENEW THE IDENTITY

A. Describe your current state using a metaphor.

I see myself as someone trying to drag an unwilling horse to drink from the watering hole.

B. Describe your ideal self using a new metaphor. Draw it here.

My new metaphor is a conductor of an orchestra. I am orchestrating the change like a conductor of an orchestra, but each team member needs to do their part and play their instrument as they know best.

C. Explore shifts in mindset required for you to move from the old to the new metaphor.

Old metaphor

- I am the only one who knows what has to be done to reach the goal.
- I need to check on the team to ensure they are doing things right.

New metaphor

- I have a sense of where we are heading and the team can collectively come up with the best steps to achieve the goal together.
- My team will own the transformation. As long as we are aligned in the vision, everyone will make the best decisions to get it right.

YOUR REFLECTIONS

STEP 3: RENEW THE IDENTITY

- Create a strong mental image of the identity you want to embrace.
- Give the new identity life by exploring possible shifts in mindset.
- Design initial actions.

A. Describe your current state using a metaphor.

B. Describe your ideal self using a new metaphor. Draw it here.

C. Explore shifts in mindset required for you to move from the old to the new metaphor.

Old metaphor

New metaphor

PRAKASH'S REFLECTIONS

STEP 4: REBUILD THE CAPABILITIES

A. **As part of your new identity, what actions can you start taking? Why?**

I will check if the team agrees with me in the direction. (Like a conductor, perhaps we need to first agree on the music piece we will be performing).

I will then work with them to determine the roles each of them wants to play to meet the common goal. Instead of dictating the actions to be taken, I will engage the team from an advisory point of view and let them decide what should be done.

B. **What might be hard to do? How can you overcome the difficulty?**

Getting the team to shift their thinking from "what we are doing is already perfect" to "we can do better" could be challenging. I will work towards increasing their critical thinking and see what additional insights we can draw. The current way of thinking is limiting us, and as an advisor, I can equip them with thinking skills to re-examine this issue.

C. **How will you know your actions are effective?**

If the team can synergize and come up with different ways of achieving our goals, I will know my actions are effective.

There should also be an increase in alignment, ownership and active discussions on how to improve our processes in product development. I should very soon feel less burdened and obliged to push things through, and there will be greater momentum as the various pieces of the puzzle start to fall into place.

YOUR REFLECTIONS

STEP 4: REBUILD THE CAPABILITIES

- Design actions that will help you actualize the new metaphor.
- Practice the actions in small steps so you can reach your goal progressively.

A. As part of your new identity, what actions can you start taking? Why?

B. What might be hard to do? How can you overcome the difficulty?

C. How will you know your actions are effective?

ENFORCING vs EMPOWERING

BENG CHUAN

PROFILE

- A senior director leading a diverse team.
- Eloquent, with high emotional intelligence.
- Had a new manager who wanted a high level of control, delegated complex work to his team directly, and expected things to be turned around very quickly.

CHALLENGE

Sandwiched between a manager who micro-managed and his team who found the deadlines unreasonable but were afraid to speak up.

GOALS

To empower his team and his new manager, help both parties succeed and gain the trust of his manager.

See how Beng Chuan navigated the paradox using the Re4 Coaching Model.

BENG CHUAN'S REFLECTIONS

STEP 1: RECONSTRUCT THE MAP

A. For what areas have you used the 'enforcing' approach? How effective was this approach?

I tried to follow my manager's leadership style in getting my team to work faster for longer hours. I got my team to prioritize tasks based on deadlines which I enforced. It was effective only for a while as the workload kept increasing and uncompleted tasks piled up.

B. Have you empowered your team? How effective was this approach?

This question caught me off-guard. I see that instead of empowering my team, I was only empowering my manager. I agreed with all he said and communicated his wishes to my team. I wasn't empowering myself either. This has definitely not been effective. My team is stressed by the workload and short deadlines, and my manager questioned my leadership when my team could not meet deadlines.

On many occasions, I was surprised to see team members working on something other than what my manager and I had earlier agreed upon. My manager had assigned the tasks to them directly and my team quietly accepted the work.

C. On a scale of 1 to 10 (*1 being worst and 10 being best*), how effective is your approach? What are your thoughts on your score?

I rate my approach 2 out of 10. This score is a wake-up call. I'm not serving anyone. My team is suffering and my manager doesn't have a clear picture of what is happening in the team. My reputation and effectiveness are suffering, and my motivation is waning.

D. What needs to happen to increase the score?

I need to help my manager see the impact of his actions on my team. While meeting deadlines is important, we should also consider how much the team can do and how fast they can operate. We are understaffed and working at full capacity. The flow of information from my manager to my team needs to be improved. I should be the leader of my team and support team members so they can thrive. I need to know who is doing what, the time required, and what we should prioritize.

YOUR REFLECTIONS

STEP 1: RECONSTRUCT THE MAP

- Discover which side of the paradox you lean more toward.
- Do a reality check on what is working (or not) in your circumstances.
- Answer in detail. If you are unsure, review the example.

A. For what areas have you used the 'enforcing' approach? How effective was this approach?

B. Have you empowered your team? How effective was this approach?

C. On a scale of 1 to 10 (*1 being worst and 10 being best*), how effective is your approach? What are your thoughts on your score?

D. What needs to happen to increase the score?

BENG CHUAN'S REFLECTIONS

STEP 2: REFRESH THE LENS

A. What is the reality for you right now?

I am in a very disadvantageous position — on the 'bad side' of both my manager and my team. My team is unable to push back against unreasonable deadlines or (seemingly) meaningless work. I am not empowering them. My manager feels I am ineffective as I am not pushing my team hard enough to get them to be efficient and to meet deadlines. I am feeling demoralized myself. I have accomplished nothing and cannot make anyone's life better.

B. How do you want this reality to change in the next 6 months?

I want to love going to work again. I want to know that I am truly making a difference in the organization. I want to be respected by both my manager and my team. I want my team to work hard, but have a say in what they do and understand the impact of the work they are doing. I also want to gain the trust of my manager. He must trust me to make the right judgment call, trust that I have the interests of the company at heart, and that I raise real constraints and not excuses. I want to communicate with my manager without fear of backlash or being judged.

C. What are the non-negotiables in what you want to achieve or become?

To be an empowering leader to my team is essential to me. I believe that is my fundamental duty to my team. I want to do my best so they can thrive.

D. In relation to your answer to Question C, what is the missing ingredient in your current reality?

The ingredient that is missing is a clear demarcation of boundaries, roles and responsibilities. I, as the leader of the team, should lead and my manager should leave it to me and empower me to do my job properly.

YOUR REFLECTIONS

STEP 2: REFRESH THE LENS

- Determine the real impact of past behavior.
- Decide what is needed now.
- Clearly describe your ideal state.

A. What is the reality for you right now?

B. How do you want this reality to change in the next 6 months?

C. What are the non-negotiables in what you want to achieve or become?

D. In relation to your answer to Question C, what is the missing ingredient in your current reality?

BENG CHUAN'S REFLECTIONS

STEP 3: RENEW THE IDENTITY

A. Describe your current state using a metaphor.

I see myself as a soldier following the orders of my commander. I was afraid of adding stress to my relationship with my manager.

B. Describe your ideal self using a new metaphor. Draw it here.

The metaphor for my ideal self is that of a bee. My relationship with my manager should be symbiotic, like that between a bee and a flower. We can have a mutually beneficial relationship, each playing our individual roles.

C. Explore shifts in mindset required for you to move from the old to the new metaphor.

Old metaphor

- The only way I can support my manager is to follow through with his wishes. I am duty-bound to agree with him.
- When my team is under pressure, I must support (empower) them by being with them through thick and thin and by being encouraging.
- I can only enforce deadlines on my team when they are not delivering on time.

New metaphor

- When my manager does not have the complete picture, it is my duty to inform him.
- When my team is under pressure, I must find ways to reduce the pressure, including pushing back appropriately so the team can function optimally.
- I can enforce my boundaries, and roles and responsibilities with my manager.

YOUR REFLECTIONS

STEP 3: RENEW THE IDENTITY

- Create a strong mental image of the identity you want to embrace.
- Give the new identity life by exploring possible shifts in mindset.
- Design initial actions.

A. Describe your current state using a metaphor.

B. Describe your ideal self using a new metaphor. Draw it here.

C. Explore shifts in mindset required for you to move from the old to the new metaphor.

Old metaphor

New metaphor

BENG CHUAN'S REFLECTIONS

STEP 4: REBUILD THE CAPABILITIES

A. As part of your new identity, what actions can you start taking? Why?

I can prepare for a conversation with my manager. I imagine he will be shocked as he has never heard grouses from my team. They have always accepted work from him without protest. They only raised the challenges to me but they never dared speak up in front of him.

I need to collect information and clear examples to illustrate my case. I must be mindful to not be confrontational. I need to think through my 'asks' clearly and request his support to empower me to perform my role well. For example, I will ask that he respects the boundaries and not bypass me to assign tasks to the team.

I will also want to ask him clearly what he needs in order to empower me and trust me to make the best decisions for my team.

B. What might be hard to do? How can you overcome the difficulty?

Given that I have always wanted to support my managers to achieve their goals, telling him that his style of leadership is not working for me is going to be difficult. I will overcome it by keeping the image of the bee and flower in my head — that we are two organisms with equally important roles.

I need him to help me succeed, which will also make him successful. I will emphasize that we are in a mutually beneficial relationship and I need his support and permission to make this happen in a way that is sustainable and rewarding.

C. How will you know your actions are effective?

I will know the actions are effective when I can have those honest conversations with my manager and my team. I will also know when my manager is on my side and wants to hear my opinions.

YOUR REFLECTIONS

STEP 4: REBUILD THE CAPABILITIES

- Design actions that will help you actualize the new metaphor.
- Practice the actions in small steps so you can reach your goal progressively.

A. As part of your new identity, what actions can you start taking? Why?

B. What might be hard to do? How can you overcome the difficulty?

C. How will you know your actions are effective?

PRINCIPLED vs ADAPTABLE

KELLY

PROFILE

- A millennial people-leader.
- Enjoyed success at a relatively young age.
- Thrived on excitement, learning and growth in her career.
- Started a new family.
- Believed that 'If you ain't growing, you ain't living'.

CHALLENGE

Increasingly bored and demotivated as the work became mundane.

GOALS

To explore ways to create meaning and find renewed purpose in her career.

See how Kelly navigated the paradox using the Re4 Coaching Model.

KELLY'S REFLECTIONS

STEP 1: RECONSTRUCT THE MAP

A. What are the most important principles, beliefs and/or values that have contributed to your success?

My principles are to live out my fullest potential. I believe in always learning and growing and that I am capable of anything as long as I put in my best effort. I have always been fearless, taking on one challenge after another. I yearn for feedback that will help me learn more and learn faster. My career and personal growth surpassed that of my peers, but I remain rooted and down-to-earth.

B. What are some positive and negative results you see as a result of following those principles?

In the organization, I am valued and trusted. Hence, I have the autonomy to decide what I want to be involved in. I have a good reputation and great influence in the organization. I should be happy, but I am not.

Perhaps this is the negative consequence of being a high achiever. It feels unnatural to continue in this role and organization knowing I am not going to learn much more. While my principles have made me successful, it also made me always 'hungry' and never satisfied. Logically, I know this is a season in my life where I can go slower and enjoy my successes, yet I feel unfulfilled.

C. On a scale of 1 to 10 (*1 being worst and 10 being best*), how effective is your approach? What are your thoughts on your score?

I would rate my effectiveness at 6. While my situation is not ideal, it is far from negative. If I persist in thinking negatively, I will demotivate myself so much my superiors will not want to keep me. Additionally, since I am starting a family, I could be too focused on stretching myself professionally at the expense of family or other areas of my life.

D. What needs to happen to increase the score?

I want to shift to a more holistic view of my life — to remember that I am living a life, not just building a career. Since it does not make sense for me to pursue other jobs at this moment, I want to find other aspects in which I can grow.

YOUR REFLECTIONS

STEP 1: RECONSTRUCT THE MAP

- Discover which side of the paradox you lean more toward.
- Do a reality check on what is working (or not) in your circumstances.
- Answer in detail. If you are unsure, review the example.

A. What are the most important principles, beliefs and/or values that have contributed to your success?

B. What are some positive and negative results you see as a result of following those principles?

C. On a scale of 1 to 10 (*1 being worst and 10 being best*), how effective is your approach? What are your thoughts on your score?

D. What needs to happen to increase the score?

KELLY'S REFLECTIONS

STEP 2: REFRESH THE LENS

A. What is the reality for you right now?

Everything is going well actually. I lack nothing. Could life be better? Sure. Does it have to be better now, immediately? Maybe not. Would it hurt for me to slow down a bit and do something on my bucket list? Sure. I've always wanted to bring my parents on a tour and this seems a good time while they are still mobile and healthy. I used to be too busy to do that, but perhaps now is a good time.

My career is sailing smoothly. Could things be better? Of course. Perhaps all I need is to shift from improving my career to improving specific processes I have control over. This way, I can stretch my team and also challenge myself to think of multiple ways to approach the same issue. I can take professionalism to a whole new level.

B. How do you want this reality to change in the next 6 months?

I want to stay motivated and continue to add value to my work. I am well-compensated and should make myself a worthy member of this organization. This is linked to my value of being accountable. I want to change my thinking of "my job is boring" to "what else can I do to bring professionalism to another level in this job?"

I wish to live more mindfully, more deeply and be more present. I also want to bring my parents on the trip that has been on my mind since four years ago.

C. What are the non-negotiables in what you want to achieve or become?

I want to keep learning and growing and to expand this principle to all aspects of my life. I am not going to rest on my laurels but I am going to challenge myself intelligently.

D. In relation to your answer to Question C, what is the missing ingredient in your current reality?

I was missing the realization that I can live by the same principle in different arenas, and adapt and update it to my current stage. What was missing was contentment too. I pushed myself hard, but forgot that the journey also involves celebrations.

YOUR REFLECTIONS

STEP 2: REFRESH THE LENS

- Determine the real impact of past behavior.
- Decide what is needed now.
- Clearly describe your ideal state.

A. What is the reality for you right now?

B. How do you want this reality to change in the next 6 months?

C. What are the non-negotiables in what you want to achieve or become?

D. In relation to your answer to Question C, what is the missing ingredient in your current reality?

KELLY'S REFLECTIONS

STEP 3: RENEW THE IDENTITY

A. Describe your current state using a metaphor.

I see myself as a tree with lush branches of average length, but with one singular branch that is very long and very strong.

B. Describe your ideal self using a new metaphor. Draw it here.

My new metaphor is a well-rounded rain tree. Still being true to my principle of "If you ain't growing, you ain't living", I want to focus on how I can grow differently and with greater refinement. Ultimately, there will be greater uniformity in my growth.

C. Explore shifts in mindset required for you to move from the old to the new metaphor.

Old metaphor

- I must learn and grow continuously.
- Being in the same role in the same organization means I have stopped growing.
- My career defines my success, meaning and purpose.

New metaphor

- Learning and growing can take place even when nothing seems to be happening on the surface.
- I can reinvent the way things are done even in the same role so that I can learn and grow.
- My life defines my success, meaning and purpose.

YOUR REFLECTIONS

STEP 3: RENEW THE IDENTITY

- Create a strong mental image of the identity you want to embrace.
- Give the new identity life by exploring possible shifts in mindset.
- Design initial actions.

A. Describe your current state using a metaphor.

B. Describe your ideal self using a new metaphor. Draw it here.

C. Explore shifts in mindset required for you to move from the old to the new metaphor.

Old metaphor

New metaphor

KELLY'S REFLECTIONS

STEP 4: REBUILD THE CAPABILITIES

A. As part of your new identity, what actions can you start taking? Why?

I will start refining what learning and growth mean to me in my context — to grow with greater refinement.

I will list all the aspects of my work where there is potential to grow and improve. This will help me increase the meaning and purpose I see in my work. I also want to redefine my job scope and set different KPIs. Once I have done that, I will share it with my superiors. This will continue to increase the value of my contributions to my organization.

I will identify other areas of my life I want to grow in and start actualizing some of them. The trip with my parents will certainly take place soon.

B. What might be hard to do? How can you overcome the difficulty?

To look for opportunities within the same environment might be difficult, especially given that I have been doing this for a long time. I will overcome this by engaging my mentors and superiors in conversations about the trends in the market and role redesigns. Thereafter, I will list a few key domains and formulate a detailed plan.

C. How will you know your actions are effective?

I will know the actions are effective when I measure my progress on a fortnightly basis. I will use my journals as a means of measurement. Some questions I will ask myself are:

1. What are the areas I have grown in?
2. What additional value have I created through the growth?
3. How is my rain tree doing? Are the other branches growing and catching up?

YOUR REFLECTIONS

STEP 4: REBUILD THE CAPABILITIES

- Design actions that will help you actualize the new metaphor.
- Practice the actions in small steps so you can reach your goal progressively.

A. As part of your new identity, what actions can you start taking? Why?

B. What might be hard to do? How can you overcome the difficulty?

C. How will you know your actions are effective?

REFERENCES

Kouzes, J. M., & Posner, B. Z. (2007). The Leadership Challenge (4th ed.). San Francisco, CA: Jossey-Bass.

Senge, Peter M. (1990). The Fifth Discipline: The Art and Practice of the Learning Organization. New York: Doubleday/Currency.

Executive Coaching Forum. (2008). The Executive Coaching Handbook: Principles and Guidelines for a Successful Coaching Partnership (4th ed.).

Dweck, C. S. (2006). Mindset: The New Psychology of Success. New York: Random House.

Joiner, B., & Josephs, S. (2007). Leadership agility: Five Levels of Mastery for Anticipating and Initiating Change. San Francisco: Jossey-Bass.

Jensen, D. G. (2013). The Executive's Paradox: How to Stretch When You're Pulled by Opposing Demands. Los Angeles: World Business Publishing.

Kotter, J. P. (2014). Accelerate: Building Strategic Agility for a Faster-Moving World. Harvard Business Press Books.

Paul, R., & Binker, A. J. A. (1990). Critical Thinking: What Every Person Needs to Survive in a Rapidly Changing World. Rohnert Park, Calif.: Center for Critical Thinking and Moral Critique, Sonoma State University.

Pink, Daniel H. (2009). Drive: The Surprising Truth About What Motivates Us. New York, NY: Riverhead Books.

Sinek, S. (2009). Start With Why: How Great Leaders Inspire Everyone to Take Action. London: Portfolio.

ABOUT YEO CHUEN CHUEN

Chuen Chuen is a multi-award-winning leadership coach who has been honored with international accolades for her outstanding work with clients in over 30 countries across five continents.

Highly sought-after, she has been recognized as an invaluable partner in shaping the leadership styles of key executives in Fortune 500 companies.

Chuen Chuen's core belief is that a reservoir of able leaders primed to lead, excel and overcome challenges can have immense impact on families, communities, businesses and nations. Having worked with senior executives since 2013, Chuen Chuen has demonstrated that a return to fundamentals — helping leaders gain deep self-awareness — is the secret to unlocking leadership potential. She has been a strategic companion to leaders fully committed to reach their highest potential as they navigate the challenges of the corporate world.

As an established and creative adult-learning expert, Chuen Chuen recognizes the uniqueness of each client and tailors learning experiences specific to each client's needs. She is committed to help clients thrive whether they are working on executive presence, influence, negotiation or stakeholder engagement.

Satisfied clients describe the coaching experience with her as "transformational, life-changing" and "the only professional development a leader ever needs".

COACHING AND TRAINING

Founder of ACESENCE company, Chuen Chuen offers predesigned solutions and coaching and training for individuals and organizations tailored to their particular needs:

- Individual Leadership Agility Coaching
- Customized Human Capital Development Solutions
- High-engagement Predesigned Programs

SPEAKING

A transformational speaker who combines clear logic and heartfelt passion with practicable action, Chuen Chuen awakens leadership thinking through topics including:

- Find the Woman Super Achiever in You
- Leadership 4.0: The 5 Inner Voices You Need to Hear
- Leading with Authenticity and Ease in the Chaotic World

CONNECT WITH CHUEN CHUEN
ACESENCE.com
linkedin.com/in/chuen-chuen-yeo
facebook.com/ACESENCEwithYeoChuenChuen

ACESENCE

JOIN ACESENCE'S
LEADERSHIP AGILITY FORCE
and unlock your next level of growth!

Designed to support and inspire leaders, Leadership Agility Force offers you:

- curated content to expand your leadership knowledge, so you stay updated without unnecessary reading
- effective support in group and individual settings, to help you stay motivated and on-track
- scaffolded and structured learning over 10 weeks — with personal guidance towards tangible results

Discover more!
Scan this QR code
ACESENCE.com/LAF

LEADERSHIP AGILITY EVALUATION CHECKLIST

An important first lesson in leadership is to have an accurate perception of the reality.

Uncover your agility to perform at your highest potential!

Access the free Leadership Agility Evaluation Checklist. Scan this code now!

ACESENCE.com/Agility-checklist

The assessment will identify areas where you are doing well and areas in which you can improve. You can also see how clear and consistent you are in your leadership brand.

Assessing your leadership agility will set the foundation for you to begin your personalized leadership development with a professional coach.

Begin your journey towards agility today!